HEROES OF
WORLD WAR I

HEROES OF WORLD WAR I

FOURTEEN STORIES OF BRAVERY

SCOTT ADDINGTON

Cover illustrations: Soldiers (*London Illustrated News*); Louis Arbon
Strange (Imperial War Museum, Q 68274); Poppy (Martin Latham);
Max Horton (Imperial War Museum, A 20789)

First published 2016

The History Press
The Mill, Brimscombe Port
Stroud, Gloucestershire, GL5 2QG
www.thehistorypress.co.uk

British Library Cataloguing in Publication Data.
A catalogue record for this book is available from the British Library.

ISBN 978 0 7509 6756 3

Typesetting and origination by The History Press
Printed and bound by CPI Group (UK) Ltd

CONTENTS

MENTIONED IN DISPATCHES

This book would not have happened if wasn't for a few gallant individuals who have believed in me and this project. Firstly my amazing wife, Veronika, who has supported me unquestionably and has never been short of encouragement or a smile!

I would like to thank my commissioning editor at The History Press, Sophie Bradshaw, for her patience and kindness in fielding untold questions and queries from me throughout this entire process. I would also like to thank my (very small, but very effective) platoon of proofreaders, Andy, Kris and Rhys, who continually pull me up on my many, many errors.

Obviously the heroes in this book are no longer with us, so I have been dependent on a network of people who perhaps knew them or knew of them during their lives. In particular, Harry Angier and Ray Verrity.

Last, but by no means least, I must thank the staff at the various museums and archives, such as The National Archives at Kew, the Australian War Memorial, the Imperial War Museum, the National Museum of the Royal Navy, the Royal Navy Submarine Museum and the War Graves Photographic Project, who have all dealt with my avalanche of email questions and telephone calls so admirably.

Thank you all!

SMA

HERO

(noun: plural heroes) Pronunciation: / ˈhɪərəʊ/

A person, typically a man, who is admired for their courage, outstanding achievements, or noble qualities.

A person who is admired for having done something very brave or having achieved something great.

The chief male character in a book, play, or film, who is typically identified with good qualities, and with whom the reader is expected to sympathise.

These are just a few of the many different definitions of the word 'hero' a reader will find in various English language dictionaries. However, these definitions aside, when we talk of heroes nowadays, invariably we are talking about an overpaid, overhyped sportsperson/musician/actor with an ego the size of a small moon. They *are* talented – mostly – and earn a bucketload of cash from the millions of fans who idolise them and buy anything with their name on it. But can they really be called heroes?

I am sorry to say this, but Wayne Rooney isn't a hero. Lewis Hamilton isn't a hero either; neither are Ben Stiller, Simon Cowell nor Britney Spears. These people, and many like them, have talent and ambition and have inspired many people, but heroes? *Real* heroes? No.

A real hero, for me at least, is someone who has been put into a situation or scenario which was not of their making, who, in the face of danger and adversity or from a position of relative weakness, displays courage and demonstrates wilful self-sacrifice in order to achieve a greater common cause. For example, the 8-year-old daughter who looks after her disabled mother instead of living a more normal childhood; the many firemen who die or are severely injured rescuing people from burning buildings; and the members of the armed forces who put their lives on the line daily to ensure we are all living in a safe and free world. These are the real heroes of today.

The First World War is extraordinary because it was the first major conflict where the normal man in the street – the bankers, miners, accountants, bakers, shop assistants, mechanics, tailors, teachers, cleaners, factory workers, managing directors, sportsmen, and yes, even some politicians – were all told to stop what they were doing, forget about their jobs, their families, their children and their homes, pick up a rifle and fight for king and country.

At the beginning of the war, every man reading this now who is single and under the age of 41 would have got the nod from the War Office. Think about that for a moment. No more driving that Audi; no more catching up with the boys down the pub on a Friday; no football; no Sky Sports; no nice suits; or brand-new trainers. Instead, you are sent to a training camp and within a few months are flung into a rather large hole in the ground that is being shelled all day long. There are meagre rations, you are surrounded by dead bodies and rats, you cannot sleep, you cannot wash and the toilet facilities are less than glamorous.

And if you are married or between 41 and 51, and feeling quite smug at the moment, your time would come in 1916 when the barriers to conscription were relaxed as the need for more men became intense. It really was social upheaval of the highest magnitude. Millions of men were put into a situation that was not of their making, where they faced almost continual danger, but just had to get on with it as best they could. Many came back badly wounded or mentally scarred; many didn't come back at all.

The men who form the subject matter for this particular book are a complete mix of personalities, backgrounds and attitude. Some were officers and career soldiers; some were conscripts and the result of Lord Kitchener's famous 'Call to Arms'; some were highly decorated with gallantry medals; others continually found themselves in trouble with authority; some were at the front for years; others were there only for a matter of weeks; some came back; others sadly didn't.

They are, however, all heroes.

2296 PRIVATE JOHN 'BARNEY' HINES

(45TH BATTALION, AUSTRALIAN INFANTRY)

John 'Barney' Hines was not your ordinary infantryman. He had the reputation at the front for being a fanatical soldier and a notorious killer of Germans. He also became a master of 'souveniring' (the collection of items such as badges and medals from dead or captured enemy soldiers); so much so that he was known as the 'Souvenir King'. He was unruly, with little or no respect for authority and, if legend is to be believed, became the only soldier in the war to have a bounty placed upon him, dead or alive, by the Kaiser himself.

This soldier's remarkable story began in Liverpool in 1873, where he was born into an Irish family. At the age of 14 he ran away and attempted to join the British Army, perhaps not too unusual for a kid enduring a rough upbringing in Victorian England. However, his mother held a different opinion about his decision and he was promptly returned home. But the young Hines was not to be denied and just two years later, aged 16, he successfully joined the Royal Navy and quickly found himself on a gunboat targeting oriental pirates operating in the China Sea.

His stint in the navy was short-lived, however, as he was struck down just a year into his service by a nasty case of malaria and promptly discharged. The malaria didn't quench his thirst for adventure, though, and once sufficiently recovered he embarked on a personal quest to find gold and make his fortune. His hunt for treasure took him all over the world – to North America, South America, South Africa and New Zealand. When the Boer War erupted, Hines was in South Africa and the temptation of adventure was too much to ignore. He signed up to the colours and served as a scout with a variety of different British units.

When the First World War broke out, Hines found himself in Australia. Despite being 41 years old, he attempted to join up. Not surprisingly he was rejected on medical grounds. He kept hounding the local recruitment centres until, finally, in 1916 he was accepted. The losses of the Australian Infantry Force at Gallipoli in 1915 no doubt caused the army recruitment standards to be lowered a little.

Private Hines set sail for Europe from Sydney on board HMAT A18 *Wiltshire* on 22 August 1916. After some initial training on Salisbury Plain, during which he was already gaining a reputation for being quite a handful, he was packed off to the Western Front in March 1917 as part of a reinforcement detachment destined for the 45th Battalion, Australian Infantry, and it wasn't long before his unorthodox method of soldiering came to the fore. Hines didn't really take to conventional infantry weapons such as the rifle (in his case it was the .303 Short Magazine Lee–Enfield rifle). Instead, his weapon of choice consisted of a couple of sandbags filled to the brim with Mills bombs (grenades). His time in Australia had obviously endeared the game of cricket to him and he would often relate his grenade-throwing exploits to his mates in cricketing terms. One of his favourite pastimes was bowling the Germans his 'Yorker'.

When confronted with a hostile enemy, Hines had the tendency to adopt a glazed stare, and because of this he was quickly dubbed 'Wild Eyes' by his fellow soldiers. His lust for killing Germans was borderline obsessive in its nature. This was down to an experience very early in his war career. Two of his mates were ordered for sentry duty in an observation post, while he was ordered back to the trenches. When he returned to the observation post the following morning, he found both his comrades had been killed. From that day, his mentality was thus — if the Germans wanted a fight, then that's what they would get, and then some. It is thought he killed more Germans by the end of the war than any other Australian soldier.

In an effort to control what was a very brave and valiant, but often unruly, character, Hines' commanding officer, Lieutenant Colonel A.S. 'Tubby' Allen, had the splendid idea of attaching him to a Lewis gun crew. Hines loved this: it appealed to his innate wish to kill as many Germans as possible during his time at the front. When testing the Lewis gun for the first time, he was quoted as saying, rather eloquently, 'This thing'll do me. You can hose the bastards down.'

As well as killing the enemy, another obsession was the collection of souvenirs. He would comb the battlefields on the lookout for badges, watches, rings, weapons, money and similar items. Prisoners were relieved of anything valuable in double-quick time and even dead bodies were not spared a thorough search. He quickly became known as a master 'souvenirer' throughout his battalion and beyond.

Hines was quickly into some serious action on the Western Front. He would always go out on forays from which he brought back almost as many prisoners as souvenirs. At Bullecourt in April 1917 he was with an officer, Second Lieutenant Hopgood, and they had been separated from the rest of their platoon. Persistent sniping from a German 'pill-box' had pinned them down and wounded his officer in the arm. Depending on your point of view, what happened next was either a flash of brilliance and daring of the highest order, or just plain stupid.

Hines had had enough of being shot at and charged alone at the fortification, screaming at the Germans inside and telling them in no uncertain terms what he thought of them (it was not complimentary). He then jumped on top of the pillbox and performed what can only be described as a war dance, taunting the Germans to come out and fight as men. Not sur-prisingly, the Germans declined his very kind offer – they were not having any of it. To encourage them along a bit, Hines dropped to the ground and threw a couple of Mills bombs through one of the gun openings. It wasn't long before sixty-three Germans came staggering out of the pillbox with their hands above their heads. They were quickly relieved of any souvenirs and herded back to the Australian lines as prisoners.

Later that day, Hines went back out into no-man's-land and destroyed another hostile machine-gun post. He was wounded during this action and spent the next six weeks recovering in hospital. During a day's convalescent leave from the hospital, he 'found' a nice horse with saddle but no rider. He promptly took it back to the hospital and traded it for a bottle of whisky.

And so a legend of the trenches was born. This legend was enhanced at Zonnebeke, in the Ypres Salient. Armed with a handful of bombs and his rifle, he was out looking for some action when he stumbled upon an enemy dressing station that had taken a heavy battering from Allied guns. He slowly entered and crept up behind a doctor standing at one of the makeshift operation tables. After a quick tap on the shoulder the doctor fell forward; he was already dead from a shell splinter through the heart. On further investigation, it seemed that the entire population of the dressing station had been killed in the artillery bombardment. Everyone, that is, except a badly wounded British soldier lying on a stretcher on the floor who had somehow been shielded from the main blast. Hines lifted the Tommy up off the stretcher and carried him off towards the Allied lines; however, the man died after only a few yards. After carefully burying the soldier, Hines went back to the dressing station to acquire as many souvenirs as he could!

When it came to souvenir hunting and collecting, Hines had no known peers in the trenches. He was not afraid to think outside the box either. At Villers-Bretonneux he somehow liberated a piano and managed to keep hold of it for a few days until he was eventually persuaded to let it go. Then, at Corbie, he became the proud owner of a grandfather clock, which remarkably he managed to carry into the trenches! Unfortunately the hourly chimes of the clock attracted the unwanted attention of the enemy and it wasn't long before his fellow Australians blew the clock to bits with a couple of carefully placed Mills bombs.

In the town of Armentières he discovered a keg of beer, which he naturally started to roll back towards his battalion. The military police, however, took exception to his actions and requested him to leave the keg where it was. For once, Hines did as he was told; he left the keg where it was, quickly got to his mates and returned to drink the beer *in situ*.

Hines' fame as the souvenir king was already well known when an official army photographer took the picture at Polygon Wood that, according to legend, incensed the Kaiser. It showed Hines with a German 'pork pie' forage cap on his head, sitting amid a hoard of treasures which were obviously once the property of German soldiers. On that day it is reputed he had amassed a huge wad of cash of various currencies, a bottle of whisky, a pair of earrings, a diamond brooch, a gold ring, several watches and enough Iron Crosses to fill a sandbag. He seemed quite unconcerned that he had one puttee missing – and so many buttons on his uniform were undone that any British regimental sergeant major (RSM) who saw him would have become apoplectic. If legend is to believed, the Kaiser himself very nearly had the same reaction when he somehow got hold of a copy. It was reproduced in large numbers for enemy propaganda purposes and described Hines as 'typical of the barbarous Australians on the Western Front'. Not that the description would have bothered him.

Obviously, the First World War was not all fun and games for Hines. At Passchendaele in 1917, his Lewis gun crew took a direct hit, with every man killed except Hines himself. He was thrown 20 yards by the explosion and had the soles of his shoes blown off. Despite this, he crawled back and got the gun working. He fired continually until loss of blood from the wounds he had sustained in the blast caused him to pass out.

There is no doubt that Hines was a tough man and a brave and courageous soldier. In anyone's book, this kind of action would be deserving of a gallantry award such as the Military Medal (MM) or the Distinguished Conduct Medal (DCM). Indeed, over the course of the war, there is a strong argument for Hines receiving multiple gallantry awards. As well as being as hard as they come, he also looked out for his comrades – he was renowned for refusing to leave wounded soldiers behind, often going out under heavy fire to bring them in. He also insisted on burying properly (or as properly as could be achieved in the middle of a war zone) as many of his fallen comrades as possible. Even after a day or two of intense fighting he would always go back out in search of bodies that had been missed or forgotten. Not exactly the actions of a barbarian.

In the front-line trenches he was worth two soldiers. However, away from the front line, Hines developed a record of indiscipline. He was court-martialled on nine separate occasions for drunkenness, impeding military police, forging entries in his pay-book and being absent without leave. He also claimed to have been caught robbing the strong room of a bank in Amiens, though this is not recorded in his army service record. Such disregard for authority probably put paid to him ever receiving the gallantry medals he perhaps deserved.

He was briefly hospitalised after the Lewis gun episode, but he was back in time to get stuck in at Warneton and Dernancourt in 1918. The injuries didn't dampen his sense of adventure either. While at Villers-Bretonneux he stumbled across a healthy stash of 1870 vintage champagne and some tinned delicacies. Hines and his mates, obviously appreciative of fine cuisine, decided to dress for the occasion and decked themselves out in top hats and tails, also somehow acquired by Hines. It turned out to be a great party, but it would be his last for a while as, soon afterwards, he was wounded – shot just above his eye and again in his leg. He also inhaled poison gas. Temporarily blind, he was sent, kicking and screaming, to hospital in Étaples.

A few nights later, German planes droned overhead and bombed the hospital, leaving 3,000 casualties. Hines collected another piece of shrapnel in his heel. But neither that, his gassed lungs nor his sightless eye could keep him in bed. He found himself a broomstick as a crutch and spent the rest of the night helping hospital staff carry the wounded and dying out of the bombed ruins and to safety.

However, the extent of his wounds were serious enough to bring to an end his escapades in France. He was invalided home and eventually discharged from the army, arriving back in Australia in October 1918. He recovered from his wounds sufficiently well to find employment in some tough occupations, including time as a shearer, drover, timber cutter and prospector, before settling down in the Sydney area looking after a small poultry farm. He became a regular visitor to the Concord Repatriation Hospital which looked after ex-servicemen, often providing free eggs and vegetables from the farm.

At the outbreak of the Second World War in 1939 it was inevitable that Hines would try to join up with the Australian Imperial Force (AIF) once more. Not surprisingly, given that he was in his mid-60s, he was refused. However, that didn't stop him stowing away on a troopship bound for the Middle East. He was found just before the ship sailed and put back ashore.

John Hines died of old age in the Concord Repatriation Hospital on 29 January 1958. He was 85.

LIEUTENANT COLONEL LOUIS ARBON STRANGE DSO, MC, DFC AND BAR

(RFC & RAF)

Once described as 'the bravest man in the world', Louis Strange enjoyed an extraordinary flying career. He was a true pioneer of aerial combat, he was a maverick and a risk taker, he was brave almost to the point of lunacy and a nightmare for any figure of authority who tried to tame him or ensure he played by the rules. He is one of only a handful of pilots to be awarded the Distinguished Flying Cross (DFC) in both world wars, and is still regarded today in RAF circles as a legend among airmen. This is the story of Louis Strange.

Louis Arbon Strange was born in 1891 from traditional Sussex farming stock. He grew up with his older brother Ronald, who was to have a distinguished naval career; his older sister Daisy; younger sisters Stephanie and Ruth; and a younger brother Ben, who was destined to perish over the skies of Cambrai in 1918.

Home during this time was the mill-house of Tarrant Keyneston Mill, situated on the River Stour. It was a working mill and, with a life that was strongly dependent on the land, it provided the young Louis with an early appreciation of hard work, responsibility, the changing seasons and the importance of the surrounding community.

Strange attended Cliff House Preparatory School and St Edward's, Oxford. Perhaps not typical schooling for the son of a farmer, and something which was not lost on the young Strange. He put everything into his education in an effort to pay back his parents. Despite this, he was only ever going to be an average student, although he was a good sportsman (not surprising given his physical upbringing) and excelled at running, rowing, rugby and cricket.

He returned home to the farm at the age of 16, where his father put him in charge of his own dairy herd and 600 acres of land. His father also gave him his first horse – a young thoroughbred hunter. Hunting was his passion and the days spent hunting with the South Dorset or Portman Hounds would always be very special memories.

At the age of 17 a mixture of this love of horses and a strong family calling led him to the door of the Queen's Own Dorsetshire Yeomanry. Members of the Strange family had served with the regiment since its formation in 1794; Louis' father had joined up in 1881 and had proved himself one of the regiment's best marksmen before returning to a life on the land.

Strange enjoyed the training and the drills with the yeomanry. He even enjoyed the long, endurance foot marches and harsh living without tents and only minimal rations. He looked upon this as merely 'fun and games', although the lessons taught here and the discipline that was hammered into him and his friends during these drills would go a long way to ensuring his survival in war over the coming years.

In the summer of 1910 his group was given the job of assisting the police in crowd control duties during the Bournemouth flying display. At that time, the concept of flight was only a few years old and the crowds shrieked and gasped in amazement at the sight and sound of these early machines buzzing a few hundred feet above their heads. It was the first time that Strange had seen a plane fly – and he was hooked.

The following year, Strange stepped on board a plane for the first time as a passenger. As he was flying it struck him, as he watched the huge panoramic view of the countryside below that the plane afforded its passengers, how much easier it would be to plot enemy positions and movements from the sky than from the saddle of a horse. He argued his views with his fellow yeomen in numerous lively discussions about military strategy. He was firmly in the minority; such flimsy and unsafe flying machines could never replace hundreds of years of tradition and history of men riding to war. Strange was convinced, however, and vowed to learn to fly and prove his fellow horsemen wrong.

The summer of 1913 would prove to be a fateful one. A nasty injury to the ribs, courtesy of an angry ewe, meant his useful contribution to the farm was cut short. Instead of just kicking around the place getting in the way, he decided to learn to fly. He spent that summer at Hendon Aerodrome being put through his paces in an effort to get certified. On 5 August, after successfully passing his flight proficiency test under the watchful gaze of two official observers, he was awarded Royal Aero Club Certificate No. 575. He was now officially a pilot.

He immediately applied for a commission in the Royal Flying Corps (RFC) Reserve. If he could get the transfer from the Yeomanry to the RFC he would spend his summers flying instead of riding, essential practice if he was to keep his certificate. While waiting for the decision on his commission he found himself returning to Hendon at the weekends to fly. He caught the attention of French aviator Louis Noel who asked Strange if he would be interested in flying for him; taking passengers up for short rides and maybe even taking part in some races and exhibitions. It didn't pay much but it did give Strange the opportunity to get some serious hours of flying in and at no cost. He said yes without hesitation, even though it meant an uncomfortable conversation with his father, who thought he was mad to forgo a safe existence on the land for a rash and dangerous life in the air.

As a professional pilot, Strange spent his time instructing other wannabe pilots during the week with the weekends being filled by either racing or taking paying customers for short flights. By the end of 1913 he was established as one of Hendon's regular fliers, and as such he was among some of the sporting celebrities of the day.

As well as racing, Strange was also becoming a renowned aerial bomber, winning many bombing contests where contestants would try and hit targets on the ground with bags of flour from a height of 300ft. Strange was convinced that such bombing in wartime, with real bombs not flour, would be of huge military significance, and he took his bombing competitions on a tour of southern England, partly to please the crowds, but partly to try and gain some mindshare within the War Office and parliament as to the potential of aerial warfare.

In May 1914 he finally got the call from the RFC. He was ordered to attend No. 6 Course of Instruction at the Central Flying School (CFC) at Uphaven, Wiltshire. Life at the CFC was pretty tedious for Strange. Flying was restricted to gentle circuits of the aerodrome and it was quickly evident that Strange was a better pilot than most, if not all, of his instructors. He was still required to follow the strict courses, no matter what his skill, and flamboyant flying or stunts were a complete no-no. That said, the rules didn't really stop him.

Convenient banks of cloud or high ground would shield his flying from prying eyes and he would often take advantage, indulging in what he would call 'proper' flying. As he was allowed to fly longer distances he managed to make flying visits (literally) to friends and family. On one occasion he was so late coming back to the airfield that flares had to be lit in order for him to see well enough to land. Flying in the dark was not allowed and he was suitably dressed down.

As the spectre of war loomed larger and larger over the skies of Europe, Louis Strange was told to leave the CFS (Central Flying School), and report to RFC Headquarters at Gosport – where he was to join No. 5 Squadron – and be prepared to move out at a moment's notice.

The call came on 13 August. Hastily, No. 5 Squadron flew down to Dover and prepared to cross the Channel. Thirty-seven machines set off across the Channel to land at Amiens. Thirty-five made it across safely and, on landing, made themselves busy for action.

Just a few days later, on 22 August, Strange was alerted by a buzz of great excitement and shouting from his colleagues – an enemy plane was flying over the aerodrome. Within a matter of minutes, Strange, with Lieutenant Penn Gaskell in the observer's seat, was airborne and on target to intercept the hostile machine. They had armed their plane, a Henry Farman F-20, with a Lewis gun on their own initiative, as at this early stage of the war the role of the RFC was purely observational. This was the first time in history a British plane had been armed with the specific purpose of taking down an enemy aircraft.

Unfortunately for Strange, his Farman was unable to climb as high as the enemy Taube, and he had no choice but to return to base. When he did, he was immediately told by his superiors to lose the Lewis gun – if he wanted to go hunting in his plane, he should use a rifle only.

This episode didn't stop him thinking about how he could improve airborne warfare. He decided that the unprotected German troops moving in and out of the lines, as well as all the supply lines, were too tempting a target to ignore. On 26 August, he set about making up a number of home-made petrol bombs and attacked German transportation lines just north of St Quentin. This small raid was Strange's idea and the results were encouraging:

> We dropped two bombs on either side of the road north of St Quentin, where we found a lot of German transport; returning ten minutes later to have another go at the same lot, we found them moving south, so we dropped down to a low height and flew along over the road, where we managed to plant our third bomb right onto a lorry, which took fire and ran into a ditch. The lorry behind it caught fire as well, and both were well ablaze when we left. It was not a serious loss to the German army, but it sent us home very well pleased with ourselves.

In October, Strange was given a new, more powerful Avro-504 plane which could fly higher and faster, and was able to take the Lewis gun into action. On 22 November, returning from a reconnaissance mission near Lille, Strange encountered a German two-seater Aviatik machine. Not surprisingly, Strange went in for the kill. After a protracted dogfight he managed to force his adversary down from over 7,000ft:

> Down went the Aviatik's nose; it flattened out over a hedge and made a bumpy landing in a ploughed field just behind a wood where the Cornwalls and Devons occupied some reserve trenches. I knew they would do their share of the business, and as it was too close to the firing-line for me to land and I had a wounded observer to get home, I headed full speed for Bailleul.

Louis Strange had registered his first 'kill'.

Strange continued to fly non-stop during the winter of 1914, covering the Western Front on reconnaissance missions, artillery spotting and taking part in random and opportunistic bombing raids on enemy supply lines. On Christmas Day 1914, when the rest of his group was enjoying the contents of the tins sent to every soldier by Princess Mary, Strange took off alone in his Avro, flew into enemy territory and dropped a football on Lille airfield, to the surprise and astonishment of the Germans.

In early 1915 Strange was promoted to captain and given command of No. 6 Squadron. It was bittersweet for Strange; on the one hand he was delighted to be given command of an entire squadron, but No. 6 was equipped with BE-2c planes which were not suitable for carrying Lewis guns.

No. 6 Squadron was almost immediately moved up to support the fighting around Neuve Chapelle, and in a few days Strange was involved in some heavy action that would result in him being awarded the Military Cross (MC). In what was one of the first ever integrated tactical bombing raids, he and a number of other pilots loaded their planes with bombs instead of their fellow observers. They were to fly beyond enemy lines and target specific railway stations in an effort to disrupt supply and communication links in the run-up to the Battle of Neuve Chapelle. Louis Strange's logbook picks up the story:

> Got a good show at last. Sent to drop three 35lb bombs on Courtrai station. Crossed lines at 5,000 feet at Hollebeke. Got hit by AA gun. V cloudy and misty, nearly got lost … Kept nose down and flew just over the top of railway right into the station. Saw a sentry at end of platform who fired as I came towards him. I threw a hand grenade just as I got to him. Rifle fire from

all directions. Released bombs from 50 feet right in the station on two trains standing with steam up on the main lines. All must have gone off as the noise was terrific, pulled machine up and looking over my shoulder saw a big column of smoke. Just missed some high telegraph wires. Made for the open country south of Courtrai, got fired on from each village, returned south of the Lys and had difficulty with clouds.

Returned back at about 5pm. It was great sport ...

Those particular trains were crowded with German troops on their way to the front line. Seventy-five were killed or wounded, and rail traffic was completely stopped for the next three days as the Germans attempted to clear up the mess. For this, Strange was awarded the Military Cross.

In May 1915, No. 6 Squadron received two single-seat Martinsyde Scouts. The Martinsyde was unstable, not particularly quick, nor able to climb very high. However, it had one redeeming feature in the eyes of Captain Strange – it could mount a Lewis gun on its upper wing. For this reason and this reason alone, Strange bagged one of these early fighter planes. His flying relationship with the Martinsyde would be interesting to say the least.

His very first flight in the new plane almost ended in disaster. A lucky shot by an enemy Albatross high over Ypres split the Martinsyde's oil tank and oil started to flood directly into the cockpit, flowing freely towards the rear of the plane, making it tail heavy and launching the Martinsyde into a spin. As Strange fought to recover the situation, the weight of the oil rushed forward, dipping the nose down. If he was unable to sort this out there would be only one outcome and it would not be pretty. He had to get rid of the oil. The only way he could do this was to try and empty the cockpit using gravity. As he tried to roll his plane the oil-starved engine gave up and seized. Somehow, he managed to nurse the plane down from 3,000ft to a heavy landing in a relatively safe area behind his lines.

His next flight would ensure his status as a flying legend. It was 10 May 1915 and he was in his Martinsyde, engaging with an enemy Aviatik some 8,000ft above the battlegrounds of Menin. Strange quickly emptied a whole drum of ammunition in his pursuit of the hostile machine but when he tried to change the drum he found it had jammed, probably due to a crossed thread. He had no choice but to stand up in his cockpit, wedging the control stick between his knees to give himself better purchase on the obstinate drum.

While trying to pull the drum free, he lost grip on the control stick and his Martinsyde, already climbing at full tilt, suddenly stalled and flipped over into a spin, throwing Strange clear of the cockpit. Louis Strange now found himself in quite a situation. He was hanging in the air underneath his upside-down plane, clinging on to the drum of the Lewis gun for dear life, hoping that he hadn't undone that crossed thread too much. If he had, he was a dead man:

> My chin was rammed against the top of the plane, beside the gun, while my legs were waving about in empty air. The Martinsyde was upside down in a flat spin, and from my precarious position the only thing I could see was the propeller (which seemed unpleasantly close to my face), the town of Menin, and the adjacent countryside … I kept on kicking upwards behind me until at last I got one foot and then the other hooked inside the cockpit. Somehow I got the stick between my legs again, and jammed on full aileron and elevator; I do not know exactly what happened then, but the trick was done. The machine came over the right way up, and I fell off the top plane into my seat with a bump …

This particular adventure wasn't quite over. When he 'bumped' into his seat he had managed to smash it to pieces, which in turn had jammed the controls. He scrambled around in the cockpit trying to release the controls, eventually managing to wrench the battered seat free and throw it overboard, releasing the controls just in time for him to pull his machine out of the dive and clear the trees alongside the Menin Road by a matter of feet. On returning to base, it is said that he collapsed on his bed and slept for thirteen hours straight – he deserved the rest.

Throughout his time flying over the Western Front, Louis Strange was frustrated at both his aircraft's lack of performance, which limited his fighting ability, and the stubborn resolution of his superiors that the role of the RFC was predominantly a reconnaissance unit and should not engage in combat. That said, he was the only one left of the original thirty-seven pioneers of flight who had flown to France from Dover just a year before – all the others were either dead or wounded. In August 1915, despite forceful arguments from Strange, he was posted to Britain with immediate effect.

While in England he married Marjorie Beath, whom he had first met in 1913 when she was a passenger in one of his many tourist flights around Hendon. The best man at his wedding was Major Lanone Hawker, VC. On 15 July 1915 Hawker had shot down two hostile machines, for which he was awarded the Victoria Cross (VC). For his first victory that day, Strange had acted as a decoy in the air, allowing Hawker a free run on the enemy.

Strange was promoted to major on his wedding day, a nice present from the RFC, and on 21 September he was posted to Fort George, Gosport, with the task of forming No. 23 Squadron. Within a week of turning up at Gosport he had gathered together forty-four men and, along with just two operational flying machines, set about training them up to be operationally fit as a squadron of the RFC. By the new year they were ready. However, a bout of appendicitis and a follow-up emergency operation to remove a swab that the surgeon had left inside him during the removal of his appendix meant he was reduced to watching his brave men fly off to France from his hospital window. It would be two years before he was to join them.

Although away from the front line, the next two years were not entirely wasted. Strange established No. 1 School of Air Gunnery at Hythe in Kent, was promoted to lieutenant colonel and formed No. 2 School of Air Gunnery at Turnberry. In April 1917 he became assistant commandant at the CFS and took it upon himself to 'test fly' the new machines as they rolled off the production line. On 26 June 1918 the call to arms sounded again and he was given twenty-four hours to get over to France where he had been selected to command the newly formed 80th Wing.

The aerial war of 1918 was very different to that which he had left behind in 1915. As with the war on the ground, and as Strange had predicted way back when, the machine gun ruled the skies. Planes were not just fitted with guns as an afterthought now – their entire design and manufacture was centred around the gun. Plane-to-plane combat, the aerial dogfight, was now what it was all about. This called for a very special personality and a very different type of flying skill, and out of the skies riddled with exhaust trails, tracer bullets and shrapnel came a different type of hero. The modern day 'aces' were revered by their relevant country as national icons and heroes of the very highest order. Welcome back, Louis Strange!

The role of the 80th Wing in this decisive phase of the war would be to scout the battlefield, to give direct support to Allied infantry attacks on the ground and to cause havoc behind enemy lines by disrupting supply lines and airbases. Louis Strange led his wing with immense pride. Although he was responsible for the administration of the wing and planning the strategies, he tried to fly every day.

Between 1 July and 11 November the seven squadrons under Strange's command, two of which were Australian, destroyed or drove down out of control no less than 449 German aircraft, as well as twenty-three balloons – a remarkable record that would lead to Strange being awarded both the Distinguished Service Order (DSO) and the Distinguished Flying Cross (DFC) for his work in planning and executing large-scale tactical bombing missions. The citation for his DSO made reference to a specific incident on 30 October:

> By his fine example and inspiring personal influences he has raised his wing to still higher efficiency and morale, the enthusiasm displayed by the various squadrons for low-flying raids being most marked. On Oct 30th he accompanied one of these raids against an aerodrome; watching the work of his machines, he waited until they had finished then dropped his bombs from 100 feet altitude on hangers that were undamaged, then attacked troops and transport in the vicinity of the aerodrome. Whilst thus engaged he saw eight Fokkers flying above him; at once he climbed and attacked them single handled: having driven one down out of the control he was fiercely engaged by the other seven, but he maintained the combat until rescued by a patrol of our scouts.

Immediately after the official ending of the war, Lieutenant Colonel Louis Arbon Strange, DSO, MC, DFC flew his battle-damaged Camel machine to England, back to his wife and to his son, Brian, who was 2 months old and had not yet met his father.

When the Second World War began, Strange dusted off his RAF uniform and got back into the thick of it. On account of his age he was not permitted to take part in active flying, but he was given general flying duties which included delivering fuel and supplies to the British Expeditionary Force (BEF) in France. He was awarded a Bar to his DFC for a remarkable piece of flying in which he managed to escape a group of six angry Messerschmitts while flying an unarmed Hurricane.

He was also deeply involved in the planning and preparation of Operation Overlord, landing in Normandy himself on 15 June, controlling local airstrips as the Allied bridgehead widened. He was also present in Reims on 7 May 1945 to witness the negotiations for the final surrender of the German Army.

For his wartime contribution, Wing Commander Strange was awarded an Officer of the Most Excellent Order of the British Empire, as well as the American Bronze Star.

Louis Strange was 54 when he left the RAF for the second time. He died in his sleep in 1966 at the age of 75. He is buried in the cemetery of St Nicolas church at Worth Matravers, close to his parents. On his headstone is the following inscription:

If I take the wings of the morning Thy right hand shall hold me …

3

CAPTAIN KENNETH EDWARD BROWN MC AND BAR

(2/4TH BATTALION, OX. AND BUCKS. LIGHT INFANTRY)

Kenneth Edward Brown was born in Kensington, London, in 1896, the fifth and youngest son of James and Primrose Brown of Eastrop Grange, Highworth, Wiltshire. Kenneth and his siblings enjoyed a distinctly privileged upbringing; he was educated at Harrow from 1909 where he was a monitor and played for the Harrow cricket XI. During the 1913 season he batted third, with an average of 16.00, and took eleven wickets for 24.90 runs each. Cricket was a sport that featured heavily in the Brown family at this time, with Kenneth's elder brother of three years, Douglas, playing for Wiltshire in the Minor Counties Championship that same year.

Young Kenneth's plan was to go on to Oxford, and as such he had already matriculated at Magdalen College when war broke out. Instead of furthering his education at Oxford, in September 1914 Brown dropped into Exeter College, Oxford, and signed up to serve his country with the 2nd/4th Oxfordshire and Buckinghamshire Light Infantry.

After only ten days of recruiting there were enough signatures for a full battalion, and although they were made up of raw and untrained recruits, a shortlist of officer candidates was immediately drawn up, of which Brown was one. In just a matter of weeks he had received his commission; he was now Second Lieutenant K.E. Brown.

Eighteen months' hard training then ensued with the men visiting Northampton, Chelmsford and Salisbury Plain, but by May 1916 they were ready to go to war. On 24 May 1916 the 2/4th Ox. and Bucks. landed in France. They were part of the 61st Division and, after a short period of acclimatisation, the battalion was thrown right into the mix.

On the night of 13–14 July 1916 the 2/4th Royal Berkshire Regiment was tasked with carrying out a significant night-time raid on the enemy trenches at Ferme du Bois. Over 100 infantry were to take part in the raid, with support from Brown and a number of men from the 2/4th Ox. and Bucks. The raid was an elaborate one, made up of ten separate raiding teams all with slightly differing objectives that ranged from capturing prisoners and identification of enemy units to destroying positions and killing enemy soldiers. Unfortunately, the raid was unsuccessful for a number of reasons, and every officer taking part was either killed or wounded. Thirty-two other ranks were also either killed, missing or wounded.

Second Lieutenant Brown went out into no-man's-land in search of wounded on several occasions, despite the whole area being swept continuously by enemy machine guns, artillery and trench mortars. He rescued at least one wounded officer and several other wounded men who were unable to get back to the safety of their own lines without help. For this action, Brown was awarded the Military Cross. The citation for the award appeared in the *London Gazette* of 20 October 1916, and read:

> For conspicuous gallantry. Hearing, after a raid, that two offic-
> ers and some men were lying wounded in No-Man's-Land, he
> at once led a rescue party of about four men, and, under heavy
> machine-gun fire, brought in an officer and other wounded men.
> He went out over the parapet at least three times.

Thus, Second Lieutenant Kenneth Brown, described as 'a great fighter and best of comrades' in the official regimental history, was the first member of the battalion to win the Military Cross.

A few days later, the whole battalion was thrown into a large offensive on the Somme. The attack was intended to keep German troops from heading south, and succeeded, but at some cost. The attack was carried out in broad daylight after an artillery bombardment that had failed to cut the barbed wire or knock out defensive positions. As a consequence, the attacking forces marched straight into a heavily garrisoned trench system, bristling with machine guns that were very much alive and kicking. There were 2,000 casualties that day and in the immediate aftermath it was necessary for the 2/4th Ox. & Bucks. to move out of the line to lick their wounds. In the reorganisation that was to follow, Brown was given command of C Company, which had suffered more than most in this offensive.

As winter took hold and the prospect of another Christmas in the trenches became reality, the battalion was asked to put together a patrol to find out whether the eastern portion of a trench known as Grandcourt was held by the enemy. The patrol was duly picked and sent over the parapet into no-man's-land. They made an immediate beeline to the trench in question, passing several bands of wire, and discovered fragments of an unoccupied trench. On further investigation, sounds and movement were heard – it seemed that a hostile wiring party was just a few yards away. Armed with this information the patrol turned around and headed back to the safety of their own trench, but after passing back through wire and over occupied trenches they couldn't find their way back, despite much groping and searching in the darkness.

As dawn broke the patrol found that they were actually 800 yards behind the front line and on reconstruction of their movements it was deemed that they had spent all night reconnoitring the British defensive lines, not the German front line! It was left to Brown, with a small party, to find out if the real Grandcourt trench was occupied or not. On a clear frosty night, Brown solved the puzzle by brazenly walking over no-man's-land and jumping directly into the trench, only to find there was no one home.

Brown was a brave and dashing soldier, and his actions and personality had been noticed at a very high level. His commanding officer, Colonel Ames, once wrote of him:

'Mitty' is doing very well indeed, and accomplished a very good piece of work at the end of last month when I sent him into no-man's-land to creep up to the German lines and see if there was a gap. He was out four and a half hours by himself, and he came back with valuable information. Later in the evening he went out several times under heavy fire and brought in the dead and wounded after the raid. The Brigadier was very much struck with his performance and made a note of it.

In 1917 the Ox. & Bucks. were in and out of the front line enduring some very harsh conditions. That winter was especially cold, and conditions for the ordinary soldier were very tough indeed. By early April the regiment was on the outskirts of St Quentin, and at night a red glow on the horizon showed where St Quentin was ablaze. Brown, who was now in charge of A Company, had been watching the show from the relative safety of reserve positions at Soyécourt. However, on Good Friday, 6 April, it would be time for Brown and his men to get back into the thick of it and for Brown to win another gallantry medal for extreme bravery in the field.

A large attack had been arranged in order to capture a significant stretch of enemy trenches. Zero hour was pencilled in for midnight. It was a horrible night with snow and sleet falling heavily, which affected the rate of artillery support for the advancing troops. It was down to Brown, with his A Company, to do the brunt of the attacking with B and D Companies sticking close behind. The men, led by Brown, moved in columns across 1,000 yards of open fields on the way to their objective. It was hoped that supporting artillery fire would be smashing the enemy wire and trenches to pieces in an effort to make it as easy as possible for the advancing infantry, as well as to keep the enemy occupied. However, the inclement weather meant that the artillery support was not as effective as hoped. The wire was not cut, as the majority of the shells had fallen short, causing more damage to Brown's men than the enemy defences. Losses from 'friendly fire' were significant.

As Brown led the attackers towards the enemy positions, the first inclination of the Germans was to surrender. However, once they realised that the British were struggling to find gaps in the wire, they quickly regained their composure, manned their guns and let the attackers have it in a big way. Despite this severe setback, Brown rallied his men and renewed his attempt to attack the trenches. It was, however, all in vain. His men didn't stand a chance against the machine guns. Before dawn, what was left of the attacking force were back in their old positions. The attack had failed.

For his action in the attack, Second Lieutenant Brown was awarded a Bar to his Military Cross. The official citation appeared in the *London Gazette* on 18 June 1917:

> For conspicuous gallantry and devotion to duty. He led his company in the most gallant manner, and personally made several attempts to cut the enemy's wire. He set a splendid example of courage and determination.

In September, A and D Companies were selected to make another (seventh) attempt to take Hill 35, and on 7 September Brown, along with Captain Rose, went up into Ypres to view the scene of the impending attack. At Wieltje they descended into a deep, wet dugout and that night listened to a narrative brought by an officer who had participated in the last attempt to capture the hill. It was pretty depressing listening to the officer talk about the stubborn defences, the numerous gun pits, the machine guns and the incessant artillery barrages. The description of a piece of trench that they were to capture and block was particularly unappealing, a 'Wide, shallow trench, enfiladed from Gallipoli (trench), filled with … Divisional dead'. Lovely.

After such a heart-warming conversation, Second Lieutenant Brown and Captain Rose clambered on to their bunkbeds and tried to get some sleep. Zero hour was pencilled in for 4 p.m. on 10 September. The night before, the assaulting troops crept out from the safety of the trenches to take up positions in shell holes on the slopes of Hill 35. There they stayed, cramped and vulnerable, until the whistles signalled the attack. At 8 a.m. the British guns opened up. Many of the early shells fell short and landed perilously close to the troops who were trying to catch a bit of sleep in their shell holes in no-man's-land. As the sun rose and burned away the morning mist, the heat of the day only added to their discomfort. Helmets were transformed into miniature ovens and huge swarms of flies (for the hill had been fought over for many months beforehand, with obvious consequences) buzzed around continuously. These, mixed with the suspense of the impending attack, made those hours sitting in the shell holes intolerable.

At 4 p.m. the creeping barrage began, behind which the assaulting troops were to advance. The accuracy of the barrage was not great with many shells again falling short and endangering the attackers. The speed at which the attack was ordered to progress, a dozen or so yards per minute, gave the Germans in their pillboxes ample time to get their machine guns going, and they did so with murderous effect. Long before the objectives were within reach, the German defenders were complete masters of the battlefield. The seventh attempt to take Hill 35 quickly failed.

Brown continued to serve with his battalion throughout the rest of 1917 and into 1918. After a relatively peaceful winter, the battalion was posted to the front line in the Fayet sector, which included the Enghien Redoubt. Rumours were rife that the enemy was planning a monumental offensive, but no one really knew exactly when or where this attack was meant to take place. During the night of 20 March a raid on the enemy was carried out; it was successful and confirmed that a German advance was imminent.

The whole might of the German Army was about to be unleashed and the 2/4th Ox. & Bucks. was going to be in the epicentre. The official battalion history describes what happened next:

Early on March 21, only a short time after the Colonel had returned from visiting the front line posts, the ground shook to a mighty bombardment. At Amiens windows rattled in their frames. Trench mortars of all calibres and field guns, brought to closest range in the mist and darkness, began to pound a pathway through our wire. Back in artillery dug-outs the light of matches showed the time; it was 4.50 a.m. The hour had struck. Our guns, whose programme in reply was the fruit of two months' preparation, made a peculiar echo as their shells crackled through the mist.

On all headquarters, roads, redoubts and observation posts the enemy's howitzer shells were falling with descending swoop, and battery positions were drenched with gas.

In the back area, the fire of long-range guns was brought with uncanny accuracy to bear against our rest billets, transport lines, and dumps. Cross-roads, bridges, and all vital spots in our communications, though never previously shelled, were receiving direct hits within a short time of the opening of the bombardment. The Berks had casualties at Ugny. Some English heavy batteries, recent arrivals on the front and seemingly undiscovered by the enemy, were now knocked out almost as soon as they had opened fire. The Artillery level crossing was hit by an early shell which blocked the road there with a huge crater. Never in the war had the Germans flung their shells so far or furiously as now.

By daylight all front line wire had been destroyed, and our trenches everywhere were much damaged. The mist hung thick, but the Germans did not yet attack. About 9.30 a.m. the barrage was felt to lift westwards from Fayet and the fitful clatter of Lewis guns, firing in short bursts with sometimes a long one exhausting a 'drum,' was heard. In the front line showers of stick bombs announced the enemy's presence. Everywhere it seemed that quick-moving bodies in grey uniforms were closing in from either flank and were behind. In the mist our posts were soon over-run. Few of our men were left to rally at the 'keeps.' A messenger to A Company's platoons, which had been stationed in support at the famous 'Sunken Road,' found that place filled with Germans. Before noon the enemy had passed Fayet and his patrols had reached Selency and the cottages.

The following is an extract from a letter written in hospital on 8 April 1918 by Captain W.H. Moberly, DSO:

I am afraid the battalion is completely smashed up. We always knew that whichever battalion happened to be in front at the time of the German assault was bound to be 'done in', and unfortunately it happened to be the Oxfords.

I myself was not with them, and that is how I escaped. I have been left out to take an NCOs [non-commissioned officers] class, and was down at the Transport Lines with Bennett. 'B' and 'C' companies were in the front line between Gricourt and Fayet, north of St Quentin: 'A' company (Brown), in two separate parties of two platoons were just behind as [the] counter-attack company; 'D' Company was in the redoubt, with Battalion HQ some way back, immediately east of Holnon.

The bombardment began at 4.30am, and included a lot of gas. This had cleared off when the Germans came across five hours later; but there was a thick mist, and the Germans had put down a heavy smoke barrage, so that, as a few survivors told me, it was impossible to see your hand in front of your face.

Under the present system of defence in depth, there are big gaps between posts. The Germans seem to have come through these, and especially to have come through the front of the Brigade on our left, and to have round behind our people via the village of Fresnoy.

The first people assaulted seems to have been [2nd Lieutenant] Brown and the two left counter-attack platoons, who were 'standing to' in the Fresnoy–Fayet road. They suddenly found that the Germans were all around them on an immense circle. Brown thereupon extended his men in an inner circle, and they fought it out until there were only about ten of them left. These then threw down their arms and equipment in token of surrender, but some of them managed to get away in the mist.

They did not know for certain what had happened to Brown, but I fear that there can be little doubt that he had been knocked out in some way or other. Of course, it is possible that he is a wounded prisoner.

Second Lieutenant Brown had indeed been 'knocked out'. He had rallied his men (or what was left of them) several times, but in doing so was shot through the left lung and quickly became unconscious due to loss of blood. When he came to he found himself a prisoner of war.

The 21 March 1918 was a bad day for the 2/4th Ox. & Bucks. – nineteen officers and 562 other ranks were casualties (killed, missing or wounded).

Captain Kenneth Brown died of his wounds in a German hospital on 12 April. He was 22. He is buried in Hautmont Communal Cemetery in France. He was one of five brothers who served during the Great War, only one of whom, Hew James Brown, survived. The others were Captain Erie Francis Brown, 5th Wiltshire Regiment, who died of wounds on 1 April 1917, aged 27; Lieutenant Douglas Crow Brown, 2nd Royal Scots, attached to the Machine Gun Corps, who also died of wounds on 13 September 1917, aged 25; and Major Gerald Dick Brown MC, 1st Wiltshire Regiment, attached to the 11th Lancashire Fusiliers, who was killed in action on 14 April 1918, at the age of 31.

After the war a stained-glass window was placed in St Michael's church, Highworth, Wiltshire, to commemorate Brown and his three elder brothers who all gave their lives during the war. On hearing of his death, his commanding officer wrote:

You know how well he had done, and how grateful I was to him for all his hard work while I was with the Battalion, and I know how universally he was loved and respected by all ranks who knew him. God rest his gallant soul.

17410 PRIVATE HORACE GEORGE ANGIER

(2ND BATTALION, ROYAL BERKSHIRE REGIMENT)

Horace George Angier was born on 23 October 1894 at 12 Vansittart Street, Deptford, south-east London. He was the third son of Frederick William and Keziah Jane Angier. His elder brothers were twins, William Barnard and Frederick William; however, in January 1894 Frederick sadly died of bronchial pneumonia when he was just 11 months old.

Young Horace, who was probably conceived as a direct consequence of his older brother dying, was affectionately known as 'Holly' by his parents and family (and as such he will be known as Holly throughout this rendition of his life). His parents were to have three more children after Holly: a brother, Edwin, who was to fight in the Second World War with the Royal Engineers, and two sisters, Norah and Eleanor.

Holly's upbringing was comfortable but not privileged. His parents obviously took considerable care to educate their boys about the perils facing working-class children growing up in the East End at that time. He was schooled at Wellfield Infant School in Wellfield Road and then Sunnyhill Road School. At the age of 6 he was enrolled in the Band of Hope. This was not a Sunday school (although he did attend one of those too, along with his brother), but a temperance organisation for working-class children, teaching them (among other things) about the evils of drink. They would meet once a week to listen to lectures on the Christian faith and other subjects and participate in various activities, including summer trips to the coast via train.

Holly wasn't a scholar by any stretch of the imagination, but he was a smart kid and a hard worker and held down several jobs in the immediate run-up to the outbreak of war, one of which was a job as a kitchen porter in a local hospital; the hours were long and the pay wasn't great, but it was a job.

The Angier family had a strong military heritage: his father had served in the 2nd Battalion Seaforth Highlanders during the Boer War; his Uncle William had served in the Durham Light Infantry in Egypt and his brother William (whose story is also in this book, see chapter 5) was already serving in the 13th Hussars and was currently stationed in India. With this kind of family heritage it is a little surprising that Holly didn't enlist immediately after leaving school. However, when it all kicked off in the summer of 1914 it seemed that every available spare inch of London was plastered with the face of Lord Kitchener telling every young male that 'Your Country Needs You'. Holly was swept up on the wave of patriotism and suddenly found himself right at the front of the queue to sign up.

He enlisted in Lambeth at the age of 20 with the 2nd Battalion Royal Berkshire Regiment. He was given the rank of private and the regimental number 17410. The rest of 1914, and indeed the majority of 1915, was spent on the south coast in training. While he was undergoing this train-ing his comrades in the 2nd Battalion Royal Berkshires were getting well and truly stuck in on the Western Front, where they were involved in some significant fighting and, if we are being honest, taking a mauling. At Neuve Chapelle, between 10 and 14 March 1915 they lost fifteen officers and 315 other ranks were killed, missing and wounded. A few months later, on 25 September 1915, during the first phase of the Battle of Loos, they suffered 403 casualties. They were pulled out of the line straight after this latest beating to rest up and refit. It was in this period of recuperation that Holly joined his regiment in the field where they were in billets at Bac St Maur. On arrival he was placed in A Company.

The final weeks of 1915 were spent in reserve, engaged in intensive training and manoeuvres. In early 1916 there were rumours spreading all over the regiment that they were soon to be moved on and shipped out to the Middle East, either Egypt or Salonika. For Holly and his mates this was good news as at least they would be warm and dry – winter in France was very miserable indeed. Sadly, the rumours did not come to fruition and the battalion marched back to the Lys sector to take over the front-line trenches at Fleurbaix. Such is the work of fate – if the battalion had moved to the Middle East, it is very possible that Holly and a large number of his comrades would have survived the war. Unfortunately for them and their families, fate was not smiling on them.

Unbeknown to Holly, at about this time he was only a few miles away from his brother William, who was currently serving in the 13th Hussars and had also heard rumours that they would be shipped out to the Middle East. This time the rumours were true and William and the rest of the 13th Hussars left France on 28 June, bound for Basra to take on the Turks.

Back on the Western Front, the first few months of 1916 were miserable for Holly as he spent most of them manning the trenches at Fleurbaix, standing knee-deep in thick mud.

Day after day the miserable winter dragged on, the guns kept firing and people died. Every day there were casualties from snipers, shell bursts, sickness and wounds that had gone septic – the commanding officers called it 'natural wastage', but for the man in the trenches these were their friends and colleagues being 'wasted' at an alarming rate. During these months, Holly at least found time to write home:

My Dear Mother

I am writing these few lines straight to you, hoping you are getting on alright & in the best of health as I am myself. We are having just as much wind as you, it is very strong indeed. Dear ma, will you send me out some 'Bachelor Buttons' I must really have some. I am always sewing buttons on & I have got tired of it so I've made up my mind not to sew any more on until I got some of those other sort. Don't forget will you. Well, ma I got your papers alright, and I had a letter from Mary and one from Harry.

I should like to be home and hear your new records. Finis.

(The post has just come in)

It brings me a nice parcel of fruit & sweets and writing paper from Mary. Jolly good of her isn't it. Also a letter from Baggors in Hospital at Manchester, I don't know if you can remember him or not. He has been wounded twice out here. And a returned letter of mine. I sent it to a chap who used to work with me at the Hospital, he is in the East Surreys. I expect he has been wounded or something, because it has got on the letter Hospital & it can't find him. Well, ma, I hope you are all well, & Dad too, sorry he spoilt his Xmas dinner. Has Dad got over his indigestion now, I hope so.

Let me know if you get the silk card safe. I sent it to you last week, I happened to strike lucky and got one. I think my debt is finished up now. Don't forget the 'Bachelor Buttons'. I am now wearing my braces until they come.

> I will close now, give the children a kiss for me, & my best love
> to all from your Loving Son Holly.

This letter was sent on 7 January 1916 while he was in billets near Serous. The 'bachelor buttons' are buttons that have a metal loop on the back which is pushed through the material and secured by a metal clip or stud. These were favourites of soldiers in the trenches to save them the hassle of continually sewing buttons on to their uniform.

By the spring of 1916, preparations all along the front line were well under way for the 'big push'. Holly and his battalion were repositioned to the south, and during May they took up their new position in the line near La Boisselle. Thankfully for everyone, the general conditions in this sector were much better than what they had been enduring. The trenches were dry and, being dug from chalk, they had much improved drainage which meant they could be kept in good condition. With spring coming and the temperatures rising the general mood of the soldiers improved drastically as they put in some extra training to get themselves ready for the big offensive, which was pencilled in for late summer.

During his service with the 2nd Battalion Royal Berkshires Holly became one of the battalion runners. The job of a runner was to deliver messages back and forth between the individual companies at the front line and their relevant command posts. It was one of the most dangerous jobs of the war as it often meant leaving the relative safety of the trench system to become exposed to enemy fire over prolonged periods of time.

There is no personal account from Holly as to what he went through as a runner with the 2nd Berkshires. However, this account, taken from an interview with 1713 Private F. Lewis of the Royal Warwickshire Regiment, gives us some

idea as to the challenges of a battalion runner in the run-up to
the Battle of the Somme:

> … the night before the Battle of the Somme … It was absolute
> chaos. I've never known anything like it. I was there with the
> Colonel, sitting right by him ready to take messages to the dif-
> ferent officers. The Front line was absolutely packed – shoulder
> to shoulder – thousands of troops. All in the communications
> trenches, the forming up trenches – they was all packed. And I'd
> got to work my way through all them to take these messages. And
> the shells and guns was going and Very lights going up – you
> never seen anything like it. All night long – you couldn't hear
> yourself speak. I never witnessed anything in all my life like it.
> There must have been thousands of guns going. The atmosphere
> was electric. It was like as though there was a prairie fire or some-
> thing – pushing and shoving. Fresh troops coming up and going.
> Well, I had to struggle through the whole lot.

During the days prior to the offensive, Holly and the rest of his
battalion camped in Long Valley near Albert, before moving up
to the front lines on 29 June. In the trenches the Royal Berkshires
faced the village of Ovillers; it was here that the opposing
trenches of the British and German lines were at their closest.
When the whistles finally blew, the Berkshires would not have
far to go to jump on the Germans. They were supported on their
left by the 2nd Lincolnshire Regiment, and on their right by
the 2nd Devonshire Regiment. The plan was for the 2nd Royal
Berkshires and the 2nd Lincolnshires to head up the first wave
of the advance. But Holly wouldn't be going over the top at zero
hour. He would stay in the trench and wait to be called forward
to deliver a message to somewhere on the battlefield.

For eight days prior to zero (planned for 1 July) the British
threw every kind of shell over to the German defences. The plan

was to smash the wire, smash the defences, smash the supply lines and smash the will out of the German Army. However, a mixture of poor quality ammunition and world-class underground German defences resulted in failure. The wire was not cut, German morale had not been broken, defences were still intact and when the infantry went over at 7.30 a.m. on 1 July, the German machine-gunners and artillery were ready and waiting. The result is succinctly described by the war diary entry of the 2nd Royal Berkshire Regiment for that day:

> Our own wire was not sufficiently cut and parties were immediately sent out by Companies to clear it. At 6.25am the intense bombardment began as scheduled. At about 7.15am the enemy opened rifle and machine gun fire on our line; this fire was probably drawn by the 2nd Devon Regt which at about this time attempted to line up in front of their parapet. At 7.20am Companies began filing down trenches and getting ready for the assault.
>
> At 7.30am the three assaulting companies advanced to attack the German line. They were met by intense rifle and machine gun fire which prevented any of the waves reaching the enemy lines. A little group on the left of the Battalion succeeded in getting in, but were eventually bombed out.

The commanding officer, Lieutenant Colonel Holdsworth, and his second-in-command, Major Sawyer, were both wounded at 7.45 a.m. This resulted in command going to the 20-year-old Second Lieutenant Mollett who, as acting adjutant, was the most senior remaining officer. With the company commanders somewhere out in no-man's-land, either dead, wounded or pinned down by enemy fire, young Mollett had suddenly inherited the command of a battalion that was on the receiving end of an absolute beating. It was not looking good; he had only 100 or so men, he had no idea what was happening across his own front, and with what seemed like the entire British front line being enfiladed, he thought better of raising his head over the parapet to take it all in himself. He had received no reports from his neighbouring battalion. He and the remnants of his regiment had no choice but to stay put and wait for orders or reinforcements.

Back in the relative safety of the British front-line trenches opposite the village of Ovillers, a call went up for a runner. Holly got the nod and he was given a message, along with strict instructions to whom he must deliver it. He was to pass the message to the brigade's machine-gunners who were located at the 'Glory Hole', which was on the other end of the divisional line, facing the village of La Boisselle. The Glory Hole was so christened due to its incredibly high casualty rate. It was a piece of no-man's-land riddled with craters and shell holes, situated at a point in the line where the British and German front-line trenches were just 45m apart. Snipers ruled this part of the line, and both sides frequently exchanged mortars and bombs. The craters practically ran from trench to trench, with both sides pushing sentry posts out into their side of the craters in an effort to guard their territory. It was not a pleasant place to be and had an evil reputation among the British Infantry, as the following description of the area from an officer of the 1st Dorset Regiment testifies:

At Millencourt I learned something of the reputation of the La Boisselle trenches. They were among the most notorious in the British lines. For a considerable distance the opposing lines were divided only by the breadth of the mine craters: the British posts lay in the lips of the craters protected by thin layers of sandbags and within bombing distance of the German posts; the approaches to the posts were shallow and waterlogged trenches far below the level of the German lines, and therefore under continuous observation and accurate fire by snipers. Minenwerfer bombs of the heaviest type exploded day and night on these approaches with an all-shattering roar. The communication trenches were in fact worse than the posts in the mine craters to most people; there were, however, some who always felt a certain dislike of sitting for long hours of idleness on top of mines which might at any moment explode. In the craters movement of any kind in the daytime was not encouraged. The four company commanders and the colonel went up to examine the trenches and reported on them unfavourably. The colonel stated that in his long experience they were the worst trenches which he had ever seen.

In the afternoon I and a companion went forward to inspect the mine craters, which my company was to take over in the course of the night. We passed down our front-line trench towards the ruins of the cemetery through which our line ran. East of the cemetery was the heaped white chalk of several mine craters. Above them lay the shattered tree stumps and litter of brick which had once been the village of La Boisselle. We progressed slowly down the remains of a trench and came to the craters, and the saps which ran between them. Here there was no trench, only sand-bags, one layer thick, and about two feet above the top of the all-prevailing mud. The correct posture to adopt in such circumstances is difficult to determine; we at any rate were not correct in our judgement, as we attracted the unwelcome attentions of a sniper, whose well-aimed shots experienced no difficulty in passing through the sand-bags. We crawled away and came in time to a trench behind the cemetery, known as Gowrie Street. Liquid slime washed over and above our knees; tree trunks riven into strange shapes lay over and alongside the trench. The wintry day threw greyness over all. The shattered crosses of the cemetery lay at every angle about the torn graves, while one cross, still erect by some miracle, overlooked the craters and the ruins of La Boisselle. The trenches were alive with men, but no sign of life appeared over the surface of the ground. Even the grass was withered by the fumes of high explosive. Death indeed, was emperor here.

The trip to the Glory Hole would not be an easy one. It was over 1km away and on the way Holly would have had to navigate through the lines of the 2nd Devonshires and the 2nd Middlesex, as well as those of the Tyneside Scottish, weaving through crowded trenches, stepping over the dead and wounded bodies, and passing the stretcher-bearers and other medical staff who were treating the wounded *in situ*. He would have had to keep his head down too; the Germans were retaliating in a big way and the threat of snipers and artillery would have been a constant shadow throughout his journey.

It would be the artillery that would have the last laugh in this instance. An exploding German shell greeted Holly as he arrived at the Glory Hole and took his life, along with those of the machine-gun crew he was visiting. Holly was just 21 years of age.

It is not known if the message was ever delivered. Such was the confusion of the fighting at this time, that the telegram that arrived at his parents' house a few weeks later indicated that he was missing. After follow-up enquiries from his parents a subsequent letter from the War Office, dated 26 August 1916, informed them that 'enquiries have been made and that it is now reported from the base that he was wounded and has been missing since 1st July 1916'. They were not given confirmation of his death until they received a letter from the British Red Cross and Order of St John on 20 March 1917. This letter came with evidence of his death in the form of a statement from Private Walter J. Shipp of A Company, Royal Berkshire Regiment: 'I know that at La Boisselle on the

Somme front, when attacking, Pte Angier went over the top of the trench and was shot by a shell.'

However, there were several inaccuracies (not known by his parents at the time) that suggest Private Shipp either got his dead soldiers mixed up or was in some other way confused. The Royal Berkshires attacked against the village of Ovillers, not La Boisselle, and Holly didn't go over the top with the rest of the battalion as he was a runner and needed to wait behind for further instructions.

A second letter, dated 6 June 1917, included another eyewitness account, from Private Hubert Hemmings, of what happened that day. It seems to tie in better with known facts and perhaps helps to clear up some of the confusion surrounding his death:

> On July 1st 1916, at Albert, in the Glory Hole, Pte Angier was killed by a shell which came over and killed all the machine gun team. Pte Angier had only been there a few minutes, having been a Runner with a message to the team. I was doing sentry duty and saw it all happen and afterwards heard enquiries made for the Runner. It was in the middle of a summer morning. The 2nd Royal Berks had a terrible time from the Germans and when they were relieved that night, only 36 left from the trenches.

The July 1916 war diary for the 2nd Royal Berkshire Regiment lists the total number of casualties of all ranks as 434 killed, missing and wounded.

Horace George Angier is buried at Ovillers Military Cemetery.

5

6507 PRIVATE WILLIAM BARNARD ANGIER

(13TH BATTALION, HUSSARS)

A restless young man who looked for adventure right from the start and found it by joining the Hussars underage, his would be a war of extreme hardship, frustration, boredom and sheer bloody terror. He endured arduous voyages, months and months of hard labour carried out in the midst of freezing temperatures of a European winter and the burning heat of a Middle Eastern summer, culminating in a cavalry charge that can stand proudly next to that of the Light Brigade in terms of the bravery of the men and horses, and the foolhardiness of the officers in charge. This is the story of 6507 Private William Barnard Angier, 13th Hussars.

Born in 1893, the suburbs of London at the turn of the twentieth century didn't hold much interest for the young William, growing up with his mother, his brother Horace (see chapter 4) and his sister Eleanor Mary. He was restless and looking for adventure and by November 1910 he had had enough of the constraints of his immediate surroundings and left home to chase down the bright lights of central London. He had no money and nowhere to stay, but that didn't matter – in fact, that was part of the adventure.

It was several days into his adventure, while he was dozing off on a bench in Trafalgar Square, that he was disturbed by a recruiting sergeant from the Cheshire Regiment who was looking for men to fill his ranks. He accepted the 'King's Shilling', as it was known in those days, and was escorted to a nearby recruiting office. It didn't take them long to discover that William was underage; they kindly gave him a meal, the first he had had in a few days, and sent him back into the London evening.

He had barely got back to his Trafalgar Square bench when he heard the sound of heavy marching boots making a beeline straight for him. It was another recruiting sergeant, this time from the 11th Hussars, a cavalry regiment. Another King's Shilling was accepted and another trip to a local recruiting office quickly followed. Once bitten, twice shy, William lied about his age and despite being underweight and undernourished he was accepted into the 11th Hussars. It was 10 November 1910 – 6507 Private William B. Angier had found his calling.

He had to bide his time for any real adventure, however. The following year was full of training – monotonous, repetitive training. He was transferred to the 13th Hussars at some point during 1911 and when his training was finally over he got the call he had been waiting for – proceed to Southampton to board ship for a voyage to India. This was the reason he had accepted that King's Shilling.

He boarded HMTS *Dongola* on 5 January, arriving in Bombay Harbour on the 27th. He finally met up with the rest of his regiment in Meerut in early February. Meerut had seen significant fighting in the mutiny of 1857 and, although that particular memory was fading fast, this area was still home to a large military footprint. India at this time was now peaceful, so apart from the usual regimental duties of guards and looking after the horses, the years between 1912 and 1914 were spent in constant training with lots of sports and recreation thrown in for good measure. They were happy days, but they couldn't – and wouldn't – last forever.

William and his regiment received the order to mobilise for war on 25 October 1914. It was Balaklava Day, when the regiment celebrated its part in the Charge of the Light Brigade. This year, however, there would be no celebrating as there was work to be done. By 13 November they had left Meerut by train, bound for Bombay where they embarked on to troopships. Loading the ships was a painful process: the horses had to be winched into the air on a large sling one by one; many of them were extremely frightened and difficult to handle, and the searing heat didn't help. But by 18 November they were all on board – twenty officers, 499 other ranks, 560 horses and one pony. On 19 November, as part of a convoy of twenty-six ships led by a French cruiser, they set sail for the west.

The journey to the Suez Canal was uneventful, unless you were a horse. The weather was incredibly hot and the horses, packed into pens under deck, were really struggling with the heat. Fighting for breath, the horses had to be almost continually sluiced down with water to try to keep them cool. The soldiers worked like slaves day and night in an effort to limit the suffering of their beloved horses. Their hard work paid off and they only lost five animals during the entire voyage. From the Suez Canal they sailed up to Marseilles, landing on French soil in mid-December 1914.

The day after they arrived they continued their journey by rail towards Orleans. The weather had turned and when they detrained they were forced to march the last 6 miles to their camp in a hailstorm. They were still in their tropical uniforms and beginning to suffer. Camp was no relief. It was perched upon an exposed hillside and the rain and hail had turned the ground to cold, liquid mud. As William tried to get some rest that night, he wished he was back in India – welcome to the Western Front …

Thankfully, after a few days they were moved to a more sheltered place and the weather began to improve. On Christmas Day, William and the rest of his regiment received a gift from Princess Mary that consisted of a pipe and an embossed brass box containing tobacco and cigarettes. This was all very nice, but William was there to fight. When would he be let at the Hun? Finally, on 12 January, William and the rest of the regiment were moved up to the front line:

> We boarded good old London buses complete with their own drivers and conductors, our destination was 'Bethune'. These Omnibuses as they were called, had the glass taken out of the windows and boarded up. They were dark grey and the advertisements were painted over. We arrived at 5pm then we were marched direct to the trenches, just in front of the village of 'Festubert', a distance of about thirteen kilometres, relieving the 6th Inniskilling Dragoons.

With a sense of excitement at finally being given a chance to 'give it to the enemy', William couldn't wait to get into the trenches. Sadly, though, his introduction into life in a front-line trench was a bit of a let-down:

> We remained in the trenches until 6pm the following evening when were relieved by the Oxford and Bucks Light Infantry. Many of us had to be lifted out of the trenches owing to being cramped with standing in the cold mud and water for so long. We all received a tot of rum before marching back to Bethune, it was good to move our legs again, it was the only way to get warm.

> Once we were in the market place we dropped from sheer exhaustion before boarding the buses to return to camp.

It wasn't exactly the experience he had hoped for. Along with the terrible conditions, the Germans were very active with their artillery and William was subjected to an almost continual bombardment throughout his first stint. Luckily for him and his mates, there were no casualties.

All in all, 1915 was not the best of years for William. The great adventure he had hoped for failed to materialise. The heavy shelling on the Western Front churned up the ground so much that it was very difficult for any kind of cavalry unit to be used as an effective fighting force, and as such William spent most of his time digging trenches in the support lines with only brief periods of front-line occupation. By November the snow came and, apart from the snowball fights, the Hussars were getting fed up with the endless digging, training and playing at infantry. Many of them questioned whether they would see any proper cavalry action in this war.

The year 1916 started in much the same vein as the previous one: digging, training and a lot of sport to relieve the boredom. All the time they were in earshot of the guns, and tantalisingly close to the action. So near, yet so far. William dug his way through January, February, March, April and May. He was fed up and bemused as to why his regiment hadn't been asked to share in the fight. It seemed odd to say the least.

In June there was a spark of hope. Rumours flew around the regiment about a potential move away from the Western Front:

> On the 17th June we were digging trenches for cables behind the lines when we received orders to return to our billets at Chessy,

a little village a few miles away from Abbeville. The officers disappeared into the mess where we thought they were going to hear of our destination. We hoped we were going to be allowed to do our bit a last.

We were officially informed as a regiment on the 19th June that we were going to Basra in Mesopotamia, a town of 10,000 inhabitants on the River Tigris, and on that day we left for the railhead at Pont Remy, which was a large station. We travelled for 2 days passing train-loads of soldiers heading for the front. I can remember that one train was full of Belgian soldiers.

On our arrival at Marseilles on the morning of the 22nd June we left the train and made our way to La Valentine Camp where we remained until the 27th June, and on that day we handed our horses over to a native regiment and then boarded a ship called 'Kaylan'. On the 28th June the ship weighed anchor and slipped slowly out to sea.

During the voyage William heard news that the 'big push' on the Somme had taken place on 1 July. Unbeknown to William, his brother, Private Horace Angier, serving with the 2nd Royal Berkshire Regiment, had been killed that day.

The *Kaylan* arrived safely in Bombay on the morning of 15 July 1916 to pick up the soldiers from the 13/14th Indian Lancers, who would fight side by side with the Hussars in Mesopotamia. On 19 July William was aboard the *Islanda* bound for Basra. The voyage was uneventful in terms of enemy activity. However, once more the conditions were terrible for the horses, and they were not helped by only having 50 per cent of the required rations for both men and horses on board, plus all the supplies for the horses had to be manually carried from the ship's hold, up several flights of stairs and through narrow gangways. For William and the rest of the men, the heat was unbearable as they struggled to pass each other with their heavy burdens. By the time they had reached Basra on 25 July, both men and horses were on the brink. But the soldiers still had to unload the ships, and during the unloading there were forty cases of sunstroke that resulted in ten deaths.

They then had to march to camp. It was 118 degrees in the shade, and each man had to lead two horses as well as carry two haversacks, a bandolier containing ninety rounds of ammunition, a water bottle and a rifle. It was no surprise that a number of the soldiers literally fell at the roadside from sunstroke and exhaustion, many of whom died.

The rest of 1916 was spent in camp, training, acclimatising to the hot weather and making sure their camps were secure from Arabs, who had a penchant for stealing rifles and supplies and cutting throats. There was very little action, apart from a small skirmish in December. It was another year of frustration for William and the boys.

The following year, however, would be different. The new year of 1917 opened with a number of skirmishes and William was in his element at last – riding fast and hard across open country, chasing down the Turkish defenders with shells exploding all around them on the flat plains. The Turks seemed to fight fair, but there was always the need to keep a spare bullet for yourself in case of capture by Arabs – they took no prisoners.

On 14 February things heated up, the 13th came under heavy and intense fire from the Turks at Shumran Bend. They were dismounted at the time and fought like infantry in the face of intense Maxim and rifle fire from all sides. One soldier had a bullet through his helmet that made a furrow along the back of his head. The next day the same soldier had another bullet through his helmet, but this time he managed to kill the Turk who had shot at him.

This was a tense and stressful time for everyone, sleep was at a premium and mistakes were made. Two soldiers were executed for falling asleep at their posts. William witnessed the double execution; it was a sight that would stay with him for the rest of his days:

> I saw two soldiers executed by firing squad sometime during the middle of February. I will never forget them. They came from the 6th South Lancashire Regiment – only young – we were all young. They had fallen asleep at their post. We soldiers took a dim view of this execution, they were good men, there was no need to shoot them, they should have had given them a Field Punishment instead. We had heard that there was an execution of another soldier from the same regiment the day before, don't know why …

Meanwhile the Allied advance on Baghdad continued steadily. Thousands of Turkish prisoners were taken during continual fighting. By early March, William and the rest of the 13th Hussars were just 45 miles from Baghdad and had lost forty men.

The 5 March started just like any other day. The brigade spotter plane was flying high above the front line and had fed back information as to the whereabouts of the enemy. On this day, the regiment was told there was a Turkish convoy about 2 miles away heading for Baghdad. The decision was made to charge the convoy, which was all well and good. However, the information from the spotter plane was wrong – very wrong. The convoy in the cross-hairs of the 13th Hussars was accompanied by a significant proportion of the Turkish Army. William and the rest of the Hussars were about to get a nasty surprise.

It was 11.30 a.m., visibility was poor and a strong wind was kicking up a dense dust storm. Through this the Hussars could just about make out the convoy, but what they couldn't see were the hidden trenches and dugouts full of Turkish soldiers, armed to the teeth with machine guns, rifles, grenades and artillery. This was not going to be a fair fight. The commanding officer ordered the Hussars to form up ready for the charge, but no sooner had they got into formation than the air exploded with enemy artillery, machine-gun and rifle fire. Still nothing could be seen for sure, but it was very evident that the Turks were out there and in some force.

The officers could have called off the charge. They could have taken a step back, remembered the disaster of their predecessors in the Charge of the Light Brigade and retreated back to the safety of their lines. However, the officers wanted their own piece of glory, they wanted to go down in history and be remembered in a similar way to those officers of the Light Brigade. In true British style they went ahead with what they called 'a glorious charge'.

With a loud cheer and swords pointing forward with menace, all three squadrons of the 13th Hussars swept through intermittent rifle fire towards the deadly trenches:

> As we came into formation and drew swords for the charge there was a feeling of excitement and fear. In the past we had trained for moments like this and now it was happening, there was no turning back. When we went forward the cheers were loud and with every increase of speed the fear left me, and the excitement grew, there was no time to think of anything else.
>
> Bullets came whistling through us as we neared the first trench, some horses dropped taking their riders with them. The noise and the dust was tremendous, with the hooves of so many horses it was like thunder and any Hussar who went down at the early stages of the charge, well, they did not stand a chance under so many horses.

As we approached the first trench some Turks were seen to run away, others put their hands up in surrender but there was no stopping now. I leaned forward and low in the saddle with my sword outstretched and as we passed over my sword went through the neck of the nearest Turk. It happened in seconds and I was on my way to the next trench.

We were now caught between two trenches, the surviving Turks firing into our backs from the first trench were bad enough but the second trench was even more heavily defended. The horses and men, my pals, were now dropping all around me and I was waiting to get mine. I could see that we were not going to make it to the next trench. On the far right 'D' Squadron had already turned out of the fray. My squadron 'A' led by Captain Newton was on the point of turning to follow 'B' Squadron when I, and my horse, were hit and we crashed to the ground among the hooves of the other horses, I received a few kicks as the other horses passed over us. There was no pain at first, the bullets had thudded into my arm and side like someone had given me a terrific punch. My horse had been killed outright and I crawled up to him for protection. The whole of my arm and side were like lead and it was now becoming difficult to move. The pain started to come as blood flowed freely from my wounds. There was nothing I could do, my carbine was in my saddle but with my arm in shreds it was impossible to use it. I lay there until darkness hoping I would get help, bullets were still flying and I could hear the groans of the wounded men around me and the occasional grunt of wounded horses as they lay dying. I was getting very worried about the loss of blood although this was starting to congeal. My other worry was getting my throat cut by the Arabs if they found me. I was thinking all sorts of things as I lay there, about my family and about my brother Holly who had been killed in France with the Berkshires.

With the cover of darkness I could see that the nearest wounded men to the trench we had passed over were being rescued slowly. Lieutenant Fitzgibbon of 'A' Squadron had gone out to rescue and look after quite a few wounded but if my memory serves me right I think I was rescued by Major Twist. This went on under the cover of darkness but the Turks were still firing intermittently every time they saw any movement from our direction.

I consider myself to have been lucky ever since we had left Basra as I had quite a few near misses on the advance to Baghdad but I was now very lucky to have survived the charge. So many of my pals had been killed but later on in the hospital I was to meet a few who were wounded like myself. I was lucky. Very lucky.

And so ended the cavalry charge at Lajj. In a moment of reflection, the official history of the 13th Hussars stated the following:

It may be noted that the loss in killed and wounded suffered by the 13th Hussars at Lajj was greater than in the famous Charge of the Light Brigade at Balaklava. The comparative nearness to England, the dramatic setting and other circumstances, combined to make Balaklava a name of glory. The Charge of the Light Brigade will always be for Englishmen one of the most splendid deeds in the history of the race. Lajj is, and is likely to remain for the nation in general, a name almost unknown. But to the 13th it will always be one of the regiment's great days, for the level sands by the Tigris saw that morning in the dust-storm a death ride just as brave and devoted as the one which has become immortal.

William eventually recovered from his wounds and was returned to normal duties until the end of the war. He returned back to England in April 1919 and was finally discharged from the army on 15 November 1922. He had served eight years and 255 days.

After the war, William worked on the trams and then became an active member of the Home Guard during the Second World War. In later years he became a trolley bus driver and commissionaire at the Gaumont Cinema in Chadwell Heath, Essex.

William Angier died on 4 March 1976, aged 83.

LIEUTENANT JULIAN HENRY FRANCIS GRENFELL DSO

(1ST BATTALION, (ROYAL) DRAGOONS)

Julian Grenfell was born on 30 March 1888, at 4 St James's Square, London. He was the first son of William Henry Grenfell (afterwards the first Baron Desborough) and his wife, Ethel Anne Priscilla. As one might have expected, having such well-heeled parents meant that Grenfell had a privileged upbringing among Britain's brightest stars and highest rollers. Education at Summerfields was followed by Eton and then Balliol College, Oxford, where only a temporary health issue prevented him from taking a degree in the Honour School of Literae Humaniores.

His literary talent was apparent early on in his life. During his time at Eton he became one of the editors of the *Eton College Chronicle* and was a regular contributor to magazines such as *London World* and *Vanity Fair*. As well as being a handy writer he was also a prolific sportsman, being naturally gifted at many sports. He rowed in the college boat and in 1909 won the Wyfold Cup at Henley. He also rowed for the Oxford University Boat Club (OUBC) coxless fours. He was a talented boxer and excelled at track and field – at Johannesburg in 1914 he set the South African all-comers' record in the high jump when he jumped 7ft 7in.

Grenfell always had his heart set on a military career. Not surprisingly, he was the first of the university candidates to pass and be accepted into the army. He was given a commission as a second lieutenant with the 1st (Royal) Dragoons on 15 September 1909. He was stationed at Muttra, India, where he frequently indulged in the noble art of pig-sticking – the hunting of wild boar while racing through the jungle on horseback armed only with spears. This particular sport appealed to his inner sense of adventure. While in India he wrote:

> This pig-sticking is beyond dreams. I can't tell you what it means to me.
>
> The rains have come, but not real continual rains; we go out on odd days to stick pigs in country blind with new bright grass, so that you gallop down a hidden well without any warning and without much surprise. I am afraid all other sports will fall flat after this.

He was promoted to the rank of lieutenant on 6 October 1911 and later that year he was transferred, along with the rest of his regiment, to South Africa. He didn't really like it there:

> The ground is composed of holes and stones, thinly covered by a rough grass called Prativesticula. Thus for the horseman two alternatives lie open. Either you fall over the stone into the hole; when all that is to be done is to roll the stone on top of you and write the epitaph on it. Or, if you are careless enough to come down into the hole and fall on the stone, they have to lift your body, place it back in the hole, lift the stone, clean it, roll it on top of you, etc., which means more work for the undertaker …

It wasn't all bad, though. While in Johannesburg, not only did he break track and field records such as the high jump but he also made his name as a fighter:

A member who was in training for the Amateur Championship said he would come and fight me. He was a fireman called Tye; he used to be a sailor, and he looked as hard as a hammer. Quaked in my shoes when I saw him, and quaked more when I heard he was 2 to 1 on favourite for the Championship, and quaked most when my trainer went to see him, and returned with word that he had knocked out his men in a quarter of an hour. He went into the ring on the night and came straight at me like a tiger, and hit right; I stopped the left, but it knocked my guard aside, and he crashed his right clean on the point of my jaw. I was clean knocked out, but by the fluke of Heaven I recovered and came to and got on my feet again by the time they had counted six. I could hardly stand and I could only see a white blur in front of me; but I just had the sense to keep my guard up, and hit hard at the blur whenever it came within range. He knocked me down twice more, but my head was clearing every moment, and I felt a strange sort of confidence that I was master of him. I put him down in the second round, with a right counter which shook him; he took a count of eight. In the third round I went in to him and beat his guard down, crossed again with the right and felt it go right home with all my arm and body behind it. I knew it was the end when I hit; and he never moved for twenty seconds. They said it was the best fight they had seen in Johannesburg, and my boxing men went clean off their heads and carried me twice round the hall … I think it was the best fight I shall ever have.

Despite being hailed as a pugilist hero by July 1914 he was ready to get back to England for some well-earned leave. However, there were rumblings of war in the skies over Europe which excited him almost as much as the pig-sticking:

Don't you think it has been a wonderful and almost incredible rally to the Empire, with Redmond and the Hindus and Crooks and the Boers and the South Fiji Islanders all aching to come and throw stones at the Germans. It reinforces one's failing belief in the Old Flag and the Mother Country, and the Thin Red Line, and all the Imperial ideas, which get rather shadowy in peace time, don't you think?

On 26 September he landed back in England – but not for leave – with the rest of his battalion he headed straight for the training camp on Salisbury Plain. It wasn't much of a training camp, however, as by 5 October his regiment was on the way to France. After some delay due to suspected submarine activity in the English Channel, they arrived at Ostende on 8 October and proceeded to Bruges as part of the 3rd Cavalry Division, IV Corps.

It wasn't long before he was right in the thick of it as they quick-marched straight to Ypres and found themselves quickly embroiled in the fighting around Langemark and Gheluvelt. Grenfell wrote from Flanders on his early experiences at the front line:

We have been fighting night and day: first rest today for four days. The worst of it is no sleep practically. I cannot tell you how wonderful our men were, going straight for the first time into a fierce fire. They surpassed my expectations. I have never been so fit or nearly so happy in my life before. I adore the fighting and the continual interest which compensates for every disadvantage. I have longed to be able to say that I liked it, after all one has heard of being under fire for the first time. But it is beastly. I pretended for a bit to myself that I liked it, but it was no good, it only made one careless and unwatchful and self-absorbed; but when one acknowledged to oneself that it was beastly, one became all right again, and cool. After the firing had slackened we advanced a bit into the next group of houses, which were the edge of the village proper. I cannot tell you how muddling it is. We did not know which was our front. We did not know whether our own troops had come round us on the flanks, or whether they had stopped behind and were firing into us. And besides, a lot of German snipers were left in the houses we had come through, and every now and then bullets came singing by from God knows where. Four of us were talking and laughing in the road when about a dozen bullets came with a whistle. We all dived for the nearest door, and fell over each other, yelling with laughter, into a very dirty outhouse … Here we are in the burning centre of it all, and I would not be anywhere else for a million pounds and the Queen of Sheba. The only thing is that there's no job for the cavalry. So we have just become infantry, and man the trenches. I believe we are getting entrenching tools, which is good hearing. We want them.

Although his time on the Western Front was relatively short-lived – he died of his wounds in May 1915 after only seven months there – Grenfell had the reputation of a man of supreme bravery and the utmost ability in the field. As such, his men looked up to him and respected him immensely.

In the days leading up to the Battle of Nonne Bosschen in November 1914, his particular part of the line was being continually harassed by a number of persistent snipers that no one could locate properly. His men were positioned right in the front line, in a wood less than 100 yards from the enemy. Because the woods had not yet succumbed to the power and persistence of artillery, the trees and bushes provided perfect hideouts, and snipers on both sides were having the time of their lives. Grenfell had asked for an opportunity to go out and locate the snipers himself, but his superiors repeatedly turned him down. However, after a few days, and after some difficulty, he finally persuaded them to let him go.

They originally wanted him to take a group of men with him, but he refused and went out on his own. Grenfell describes what happened on his trip out into no-man's-land:

Off I crawled through the sodden clay and trenches, going about a yard a minute, and listening and looking as I thought it was not possible to look and listen. I went out to the right of our lines, where the 10th were, and where the Germans were nearest. I took about thirty minutes to do thirty yards; then I saw the Hun trench, and I waited there a long time, but could see or hear nothing. It was about ten yards from me. Then I heard some Germans talking, and saw one put his head up over some bushes, about ten yards behind the trench. I could not get a shot at him I was too low down, and of course I could not get up. So I crawled on again very slowly to the parapet of their trench. It was very exciting. I was not sure that there might not have been someone there, or a little further along the trench. I peeped through their loop-hole and saw nobody in the trench. Then the German behind put his head up again. He was laughing and talking; I saw his teeth glistening against my foresight and I pulled the trigger very slowly. He just grunted and crumpled up. The others got up and whispered to each other. I do not know which were most frightened, them or me. I think there were four or five of them. They could not trace the shot; I was flat behind the parapet and hidden. I just had the nerve not to move a muscle and stay there. My head was fairly hammering. They did not come forward and I could not see them as they were behind some bushes and trees, so I crept back inch by inch. About sixty yards off I found their trench again. Then a single German came through the woods towards the trench. I saw him fifty yards off. He was coming along, upright and careless, making a great noise. I heard him before I saw him. I let him get within twenty-five yards, and shot him in the heart. He never made a sound. Nothing for ten minutes, and then there was a noise and talking, and a lot of them came along through the wood behind the trench about forty yards from me. I counted about twenty and there were more coming. They halted in front, and I picked out the one I thought was the officer, or sergeant. He stood facing the other way, and I had a steady shot at him behind the shoulders. He went down, and that was all I saw. I went back at a sort of galloping crawl to our lines and sent a message to the 10th that the Germans were moving up their way in some numbers. Half an hour afterwards they attacked the 10th and our right in massed formations, advancing slowly to within ten yards of the trenches. We simply mowed them down. It was rather horrible … the 10th told me in the evening that they counted 200 dead in a little bit of the line, and the 10th and us only lost ten.

He was brave, there was no question, but he was also unassuming and shied away from attention or glory:

They have made quite a ridiculous fuss about me stalking and getting the message through. I believe they are going to send me up to our general and all sorts.

That trip to the general proved quite fruitful, as Lieutenant Grenfell was mentioned in dispatches on 20 November by Field Marshal Lord French and on 1 January 1915 the *London Gazette* announced that he was to be made a Companion of the Distinguished Service Order. The citation for this award read:

On the 15th November, he succeeded in reaching a point behind the enemy's trenches and making an excellent reconnaissance, furnishing early information of an impending attack by the enemy.

Grenfell was promoted to the rank of captain on 10 December 1914 and was once more mentioned in Lord French's dispatches of 14 January 1915. He was most definitely one of the brightest stars of the British Army and had a promising future in front of him.

During the winter of 1914–15 the bad weather put paid to either side mounting any kind of serious offensive. The days were passed by improving trenches, reinforcing defensive positions, building communication lines and making plans for the spring. During some of this quiet time Grenfell found the time to put pen to paper and turn his thoughts and experiences of the last few months into prose. One such poem, called 'Into Battle', was written in April 1915 and one critic called it 'one of the swell things in English literature'.

The poem was sent to *The Times*, but before they had time to print it he was seriously wounded. On 12 May 1915 Grenfell and his regiment found themselves 500 yards behind the line in their role as chief support to a planned attack on the German lines in the area around Hooge Lake. His battalion was dug in behind a small hill, which the Germans were shelling to pieces (that hill quickly gained the nickname 'the little hill of death'). During the bombardment Grenfell went down to the lookout post and had a lucky escape with a shell that knocked him clean over but did no physical damage.

He then volunteered to go across to the front line, held by the Somerset Yeomanry, to report on his findings and observations. Despite murderous artillery fire, he successfully returned to his own lines after filling in the officers at the front. On his return, he went for a walk with his general to discuss the overall situation when a shell burst just a matter of yards from them, knocking them both over and wounding Grenfell in the head. His general carried him down towards the safety of the trenches and was wounded doing so. Grenfell was carried to the casualty clearing station by his fellow officers and when he arrived he asked the doctor if he was going to die, adding, 'I only want to know, I am not in the least bit afraid.'

He was later sent to hospital in Boulogne where he was met by his sister and his parents. In hospital, when the doctor asked him how long he was unconscious after he was hit, Grenfell replied with typical gusto, 'I was up before the count!' Julian Grenfell died of his wounds during the afternoon of 26 May. He was 27 years of age and is buried in Boulogne Eastern Cemetery. On the day his death was announced, his poem 'Into Battle' appeared in *The Times*. It was at once recognised as one of the finest of the many fine poems inspired by the war. Sir Walter Raleigh wrote of it:

> I don't think that any poem ever embodied soul so completely ...
> Those who glorified War had always, before this, been a little too
> romantic; and those who had a feeling for the reality of War had
> always been a little too prosaic. It can't be done again.

Into Battle

The naked earth is warm with spring,
And with green grass and bursting trees
Leans to the sun's gaze glorying,
And quivers in the sunny breeze;
And life is colour and warmth and light,
And a striving evermore for these;
And he is dead who will not fight;
And who dies fighting has increase.

The fighting man shall from the sun
Take warmth, and life from the glowing earth;
Speed with the light-foot winds to run,
And with the trees to newer birth;
And find, when fighting shall be done,
Great rest, and fullness after dearth.

All the bright company of Heaven
Hold him in their high comradeship,
The Dog-Star, and the Sisters Seven,
Orion's Belt and sworded hip.

The woodland trees that stand together,
They stand to him each one a friend;
They gently speak in the windy weather;
They guide to valley and ridge's end.

The kestrel hovering by day,
And the little owls that call by night,
Bid him be swift and keen as they,
As keen of ear, as swift of sight.

The blackbird sings to him, 'Brother, brother,
If this be the last song you shall sing,
Sing well, for you may not sing another;
Brother, sing.'

In dreary, doubtful, waiting hours,
Before the brazen frenzy starts,
The horses show him nobler powers;
O patient eyes, courageous hearts!

And when the burning moment breaks,
And all things else are out of mind,
And only joy of battle takes
Him by the throat, and makes him blind,
Through joy and blindness he shall know,
Not caring much to know, that still
Nor lead nor steel shall reach him, so
That it be not the Destined Will.

The thundering line of battle stands,
And in the air death moans and sings;
But Day shall clasp him with strong hands,
And Night shall fold him in soft wings.

John Hines with his souvenirs from the fighting at Polygon Wood, Belgium.
(Australian War Memorial, E00822)

Louis Arbon Strange.
(Imperial War Museum,
Q 68274)

Kenneth Edward Brown.
(From *Harrow Memorials
of the Great War*, Vol. VI,
printed for Harrow School
by Philip Lee Werner,
publisher to the Medici
Society, Ltd)

Horace George Angier. (Courtesy of Harry Angier)

Graham Seton Hutchison by Bassano (taken 24 October 1929). (© National Portrait Gallery, London)

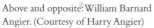

Above and opposite: William Barnard
Angier. (Courtesy of Harry Angier)

Above right: Julian Henry Francis
Grenfell. (From *Julian Grenfell: His Life
and the Times of his Death 1888–1915* by
Nicholas Moseley, by permission of
Weidenfeld & Nicholson)

IN LOVING MEMORY OF
GEOFFREY CLAUDE
LANGDALE OTTLEY D.S.O.
LIEUTENANT SCOTS GUARDS
ONLY SON OF
REAR ADMIRAL SIR CHARLES and LADY OTTLEY
OF CORNAHAN LODGE.
BORN JANUARY 20TH 1896
DIED DECEMBER 21ST 1914, AT BOULOGNE
OF WOUNDS RECEIVED IN ACTION
ON DECEMBER 18TH WHEN LEADING AN ATTACK
ON THE GERMAN TRENCHES NEAR LILLE
AGED 18 3/4 YEARS

BLESSED ARE THE PURE IN HEART, FOR THEY SHALL SEE GOD.

Resting place of Geoffrey Claude Langdale Ottley. (The War Graves Photographic Project (in association with the CWGC))

Hubert William Godfrey Jones. (Royal
Aero Club Trust)

Max Horton. (Imperial War Museum, A 20789)

7

COMMANDER MAX KENNEDY HORTON GCB, DSO AND TWO BARS

(ROYAL NAVY)

Max Kennedy Horton was born on 29 November 1883 in Rhosneigr, a small Welsh village on the west coast of Anglesey. He was the second son of a family of four to Robert Joseph Angel Horton and Esther Maud Horton. His father was a member of the London Stock Exchange and his mother's family also had a tradition of work in the City. Shortly before he was born his parents moved out to Wales, buying the Maelog Lake Hotel. It was here that Max and his older brother D'Arcy would do the majority of their growing up.

Luckily for them, they had each other, as many of the local Welsh neighbourhood looked upon them as foreigners and didn't have much to do with them or the rest of the Horton family. The brothers attended various schools on the English–Welsh border, where Max worked hard and excelled at most subjects, especially mathematics.

From an early age he had decided that he wanted to go into the navy. He told his mother at the age of 9 that he wanted to do it so he could fight for her. He had no difficulty passing into HMS *Britannia* (Dartmouth) on 15 September 1898, just shy of his 15th birthday. At Dartmouth he won the middle-weight boxing championship and broke into the first team at football. His love for football – rather than rugby, the traditional sport of officers – stayed with him throughout and was one of many reasons he would always enjoy a close relationship with the rank and file on his ships, regardless of his own lofty position.

He was a lover of new gadgets and machinery, and he also longed for the opportunity to lead and be in charge of his own destiny. He had always had an uneasy relationship with authority and longed for the opportunity to do things his own way. These two drivers were instrumental in turning his thoughts and attention to the new submarine branch of the navy, which was currently in its embryonic stages of development. Unlike the traditional branches of the navy, with submarines the command of a boat could come at a much earlier age and there was plenty of scope for getting involved with new ideas and strategies of warfare with this new technology. In October 1904, Horton was appointed sub lieutenant to HMS *Thames*, the depot ship for the training of submariners.

On 16 June 1907, aged just 22 and shortly after being promoted to lieutenant, Horton was given command of A1, a new submarine of 200 tonnes, salvaged and refurbished after being sunk in 1904 to be used for training and experimental purposes. In October 1907 his commanding officer wrote this report on him:

M. K. Horton.

Good at his boat and bad socially.

Made very good attacks in A.1. Always supposed to be very good at the engine.

A boxer and footballer – desperate motor-cyclist.

Troublesome in the mess – insubordinate to First Lieutenant. Bad
language but extremely intelligent.

At this time, there was considerable opposition to the continued development of submarines, both from the Admiralty
and from parliament. In those early days the members of the
submarine service were looked upon as nothing more than
a bunch of pirates in the eyes of many of the more senior
figures in the old navy establishment. In a bid to tame some of
the more flamboyant characters in the submarine service (of
which Horton was one), the Lords of the Admiralty decided
that submarine officers with the rank of lieutenant must spend
at least two years serving on surface ships to gain experience
in general service conditions, and so in early 1910 Lieutenant
Horton was posted to the cruiser *Duke of Edinburgh*.

His two years on board were a bit tedious; that is, until
13 December 1911, just a few weeks before he was due to
return to the submarines. A wireless message reached the
Duke of Edinburgh that the P&O liner *Delhi* had run aground
on a reef off Cape Spartel at the mouth of the Mediterranean.
The *Duke of Edinburgh* rushed to the scene and, in the middle
of a huge gale and biblical rain, Horton managed to get a
boat to the scene of the wreck and rescue some passengers.
With the help of a French cruiser and the battleship *London*
all the passengers were safely transferred to waiting ships. For
his personal exploits in this rescue he was awarded the Silver
Board of Trade Medal for Saving Life at Sea.

On returning to the submarines after his stint on board
traditional ships, Horton was given the command of D6. His
career continued to progress steadily and by 1912 he held the
rank of lieutenant commander.

During the summer of 1914, with the threat of war
menacingly close, Horton took charge of submarine E9.

At 800 tonnes it was one of the very first ocean-going British submarines. At the very beginning of the war, in summer 1914, the Royal Navy was on high alert, patrolling the high seas for any hint of the enemy. Mining of the sea highways was a German speciality and the Royal Navy submarines had an important role to play in keeping the much-needed merchant routes open in order to feed not just the British population, but also an insatiable war machine.

Horton was commanding the British submarine E9 in the Heligoland region. He had been in the thick of it during the Battle of Heligoland Blight, but had not had the opportunity to strike at any enemy ships. However, that was all about to change. On 13 September E9 was on a routine patrol in the area of Heligoland, not so much proactively looking out for enemy ships to sink but to reconnoitre the area and monitor enemy activity, when all of a sudden a small German cruiser appeared on the horizon, approaching them from the direction of Wilhelmshaven. There was great excitement on board E9; it was rare to see an enemy ship, even so close to the German coastline.

The decision to engage was a no-brainer. Horton ordered his men to their battle stations and, with his periscope a few inches above the surface, watched with excitement and anticipation as the enemy vessel slowly approached, seemingly without a care in the world. It was the light cruiser *Hela*, and she was about to get the shock of her life. To be honest, she was not exactly the pride of the Imperial German Fleet. She was a 2,000-tonne vessel that had been launched in 1895 but had undergone a significant refit just a few years ago and was working as a dispatch ship within the Imperial German Fleet. Horton downed the periscope and dived for a brief period of time, before gingerly raising it once more to track the *Hela*. There she was, well within range and carrying on her merry way, not one of her passengers had a clue as to what was about to hit them.

After a final check of bearings and a last look at the doomed vessel, Horton barked out his orders: 'Fire bow torpedoes and dive!' It was 6.30 a.m. There followed an intense surge of movement and action from the crew. Adrenalin took over the submarine as every man worked their allotted part of the process to perfection. Then silence – all ears straining as they waited for the muffled confirmation of a hit.

They didn't have long to wait. Less than a minute later they heard a subdued boom and a small current of water rocked the submarine gently to give a secondary confirmation. At least one of the torpedoes had hit their target. Resisting the urge to surface, E9 stayed submerged for fifteen minutes. When she crept up near enough to allow the use of the periscope, Horton could see that *Hela* was in a lot of trouble. She had a severe list to starboard and was already evacuating crew to other ships that had come to her rescue and to search for the culprit.

With that in mind, Horton quickly dived again to evade their search. After what seemed an eternity to the crew, E9 surfaced once more. *Hela* had completely disappeared. However, the German destroyers hadn't, and they were scouring the area for any British submarine. It was time to get out of there, but part of Horton's orders were to examine the outer anchorage of Heligoland – a task he carried out twenty-four hours later at considerable risk, as there was a large amount of enemy activity still in the area.

Eventually, Horton and E9 inched their way back to the relative safety of British waters and arrived home in Harwich flying the Jolly Roger flag, a tongue-in-cheek riposte at the naval hierarchy who viewed submariners as little more than pirates. (The tradition of submarines flying the Jolly Roger after a successful campaign continues to this day.)

A few weeks later, E9 was in the thick of it once more when patrolling near the River Ems estuary, just off the strategically important port of Emden. It was a difficult and frustrating tour as the area was swarming with destroyers, but there were no big battleships for them to have a go at. On the last day of their patrol, after failing to see any decent target for the duration of the tour, Horton decided to settle a score with one of the destroyers that had been hounding him for the past few days. It was 6 October 1914.

Horton took E9 to the seabed and waited. All the crew could do was sit there and listen to the echoing of the destroyer's engines as they prowled the area and the rattling and crashing of their snares and traps as they searched for the submarine. The tension was unbearable, as they expected any second to get snared and either pitched upside down or blown to kingdom come. After what seemed an eternity, the ghostly sounds faded away and cautiously Horton inched his submarine close enough to the surface to enable the use of his periscope. He spotted two enemy destroyers within close range: one was rattling along at a fair rate of knots, the other seemed to be going much more slowly. Horton sensed an opportunity to stick two fingers up at the Imperial German Navy and immediately gave the orders to engage the slower boat. Within a matter of seconds they were heading straight for it with a single intention – destroy the destroyer.

Another round of orders and E9 dived and let rip with a torpedo. Within seconds the crew were rewarded with the muted sound of an explosion as the torpedo crashed into the side of the destroyer. The enemy ship had been hit square amidships, and was literally cut into two. By the time Horton had surfaced to view the wreckage there was nothing visible apart from the forward end of the bow pointing skyward.

The enemy ship in question was the destroyer S126, launched in 1903 and carrying a crew of about eighty officers and crew, most of whom perished in this incident. Horton and the crew of E9 had claimed their second victim, and Horton himself was gaining quite a reputation. When Horton steered E9 safely back to Harwich he was flying *two* Jolly Roger flags. The other submariners loved it – and so did the press.

The two actions combined were mentioned in the dispatch, dated 17 October 1914, of Commodore Roger J.B. Keyes, CB, MVO:

> On the 13th September E9 (Lieut-Commander Max K. Horton) torpedoed and sank the German light cruiser Hela six miles south of Heligoland. A number of destroyers were evidently called to the scene after E9 had delivered her attack, and three hunted her for several hours. On the 14th Sept., in accordance with his orders, Lieut-Commander Horton examined the outer anchorage of Heligoland, a service attended by considerable risk … On 6th Oct., E9 (Lieut-Commander Max K. Horton), when patrolling off the Ems, torpedoed and sank the enemy's destroyer S126. The enemy's torpedo craft pursued tactics, which, in connection with their shallow draft, make them exceedingly difficult to attack with torpedo, and Lieut-Commander Horton's success was the result of much patient and skilful zeal. He is a most enterprising submarine officer, and I beg to submit his name for favourable consideration.

The submission was indeed favourable, for his actions, Commander Horton was appointed to be a Companion of the Distinguished Service Order. The appointment was published in the same *London Gazette* issue as the above dispatch on 23 October 1914.

However, Horton had little time to enjoy his success on dry land. He was asked to transfer to the Baltic, with orders to disrupt German supplies from Sweden and generally give assistance to Russia against a strong German presence in this area. By 18 October 1914, E9 was patrolling the Baltic on the lookout for likely targets. Horton didn't hang about and by the time the ice had started to encroach on to the sea routes he had managed to sink a number of merchant ships carrying supplies from Sweden.

When winter finally set in, he was expected to return to base. However, he took E9 out to sea on a test trip to push himself, the boat and the crew as far as he could. He wanted to know the limits of submarine warfare in a wintry Baltic Sea. During their test voyage, spray froze and formed ice up to 6in thick over the exterior. In order to dive, the crew had to continually remove ice from the conning tower so that it could be closed in an emergency. When he dived, the warmer salt water helped free the submarine from much of the ice.

His enterprising work in the early stages of the conflict had not gone unnoticed at the Admiralty and he was duly promoted to commander on New Year's Eve 1914. The submarine activity in the Baltic Sea continued throughout 1915 amid tight security and secrecy, and Horton contin-ued to have success after success. On 2 July 1915, when a small German fleet was cruising off the Gulf of Danzig, Commander Horton happened to be in the same area. This was unfortunate for the Germans, who subsequently lost one of their best pre-Dreadnought battleships with a loss of 736 officers and men. The results achieved by E9 and the other submarines took its toll on the German war effort and more submarines were sent to the area. Russia was very pleased, and when Horton was requested to return to England for service in new submarines in home waters, they asked if Horton could stay in the Baltic as senior naval officer at the newly formed British Baltic Bridge. The response from the second sea lord, written in a naval docket at headquarters was short and to the point: 'I understand Commander Horton is something of a pirate and not at all fitted for the position of S.N.O. in the Baltic.'

For his services in Russia, Commander Horton was awarded a Bar to his DSO, the confirmation of which appeared in the supplement to the *London Gazette* on 2 November 1917. To add to his growing tally of awards, the Russians bestowed upon him the Order of St Vladimir with Swords, the Order of St Ann with Swords and Diamonds, and the Order of St George. In addition to these, the French government made him a Chevalier of the Légion d'honneur for gallantry in attacking enemy warships.

Horton travelled back to England from Russia by train, under false documents and in civilian clothing. On 25 January 1916 he was given command of a new submarine – J6 was 1,200 tonnes and straight out of the box. He then spent the next eighteen months in defensive duties patrolling the North Sea and keeping tabs on the enemy fleet. In an age where air reconnaissance had not evolved to the levels required to launch reliable air patrols, it was down to the submarines to feed the Admiralty with news of hostile movements. Not exactly edge of the seat stuff, but important nonetheless.

At the end of 1916, Horton was asked to supervise the building and command of a new experimental submarine, the M1. The M1 was a significant departure from previous submarine designs with, among other things, a 12in gun mounted to the turret. Although it passed the initial tests and was entered into operational service, M1 never saw action.

The end of the war didn't mean the end of patrols for the navy. Early in 1919 Horton, and many other seamen who were looking forward to a rest after four long years of conflict, were packed off to the Baltic to assist against Bolshevik aggression.

This time, Horton was in charge of a submarine flotilla and didn't return to England until the spring of 1920. Commander Horton was awarded a second Bar to his DSO, 'For distinguished services in command of the Third Submarine Flotilla and as Senior Naval Officer, Reval'. This award was officially announced in the supplement to the *London Gazette* on 8 March 1920.

In June 1920 Horton was promoted to captain and a month later was given the position of chief staff officer to Rear Admiral Submarines Douglas Dent. He was 37 years of age. Not bad going ... for a pirate.

During the interwar years, Horton's career continued to move onwards and upwards. On 17 October 1932 he was promoted to rear admiral, and on 19 August 1936 he was promoted to vice admiral. In the summer of 1937 he was given command of the reserve fleet, consisting of around 140 ships of all shapes and sizes, based in docks and ports around the British coast. By the summer of 1939 the reserve fleet was in fighting shape and ready to sail when given the nod.

When war eventually broke out with Germany in 1939, Horton became Vice Admiral Northern Patrol, entrusted with the task of enforcing a distant blockade of Germany by intercepting merchant ships of all types between Scotland and Iceland. These roles were all well and good, but deep down Horton wanted a bit more action, and his prayers were answered in 1940 when he was appointed Vice Admiral Submarines commanding all home-based submarines.

Although technically too senior to hold this role, the Admiralty were of the opinion that this post needed someone who had commanded submarines with distinction in the previous war – and Horton fitted the bill perfectly. Naturally, Horton was delighted with this appointment, writing to a friend:

The new job is taking over the Submarine Branch again …
Always told you when things got bad I hoped they would send
for me, and it looks like they have done it. I am so happy, happy,
happy at the prospect of what lies ahead. I am almost falling over
myself with excitement.

Twelve months after Horton had taken over the control of
the home submarine fleet, it was clear that the chance of a
seaborne invasion of Britain by Nazi Germany was becoming
more and more remote. Hitler had failed to take control of the
skies above the English Channel, and had failed to take control of the Channel itself, in no small part down to the dogged
determination of the home-based submarines who hounded
and hunted every enemy ship that came even remotely close
to Britain's shores.

Promoted to admiral on 9 January 1941, Horton was
appointed Commander-in-Chief Western Approaches
on 17 November 1942. During the Battle of the Atlantic,
Horton was instrumental in instituting a number of tactical
changes, both in the way naval convoys were arranged and
how naval and air forces were organised. He achieved near
perfect co-operation between the warships and aircraft under
his command to preserve the merchant ships and destroy the
U-boats. As a direct result, the tide of the battle slowly turned
in his favour.

After the war, Horton was awarded the GCB (Knight
Grand Cross of the Most Honourable Order of the Bath)
and various other civic awards, including the Freedom of the
City of Liverpool. On 16 October 1945, he was placed on
the retired list at his own request to enable the progression of
younger officers.

Admiral Sir Max Horton died from coronary thrombosis
on 30 July 1951, aged 67. His ashes were scattered at sea.

8

LIEUTENANT GEOFFREY CLAUDE LANGDALE OTTLEY DSO

(2ND BATTALION, SCOTS GUARDS)

Geoffrey Ottley was not even 19 years of age when he was mortally wounded on the parapet of the German trenches as he rallied his men in a daylight attack. His story is somewhat typical of thousands of young officers drafted into the British Army for the war effort. Lieutenant Ottley served at the front for just six weeks but in that short time, he grew from an inexperienced schoolboy to an effective leader who looked after and inspired his men. Although he did not live to receive it personally, it is thought he was the youngest recipient of the Distinguished Service Order (DSO) during the First World War.

Geoffrey Ottley was born in Southsea, Hampshire, on 20 January 1896. He was the only child of Rear Admiral Sir Charles Langdale Ottley, KCMG, CB, MVO and Lady Ottley, daughter of Colonel Alexander Stuart, RA. The family were based in Fort William and central London, and his early years were split between the two family homes.

He was educated at Harrow and, bearing in mind his family lineage and background, it was no surprise that he was knocking on the door of the Royal Military College at Sandhurst in February 1914, passing out first from his group of cadets and obtaining a prize cadetship. During that first few months at Sandhurst he excelled, but, during a brief summer break in which he travelled back to his family home in Scotland, it was becoming more and more evident that a European war was very close. He quickly returned to Sandhurst with a spring in his step, eagerly awaiting the prospect of seeing some active service.

He didn't have to wait long. On 1 October he was granted a commission with the Scots Guards, joining them as a second lieutenant. But, to his great disappointment, he was not immediately ushered off to France. Instead, he remained in England, taking part in ceremonial drills and parades at Buckingham Palace and St James. Glamourous it may have been, but Ottley wanted to fight, and after a month or so he started to get restless. Fortunately however, on 7 November he got the news he was waiting for. He received the order to move out, along with seven other officers and 250 men earmarked to replace casualties from the 2nd Battalion, Scots Guards, who had been fighting admirably at Ypres during October.

He arrived on 11 November and within a few days his battalion was occupying front-line trenches near Sailly. The weather was not great and his initiation to trench warfare was pretty miserable. Snow and heavy frost meant that many men suffered with frostbite, but his cheerful disposition and the way in which he made light of the difficulties they were facing quickly made him many friends. He was very much at home at the front – he loved it. In a letter home he wrote, 'If I were brought home by force I should be absolutely wretched until I got back here again into the cold and wet.'

He quickly became very comfortable with commanding men and it didn't take him long to gain the respect and admiration of his fellow officers and the men under him.

His light-hearted attitude, courage and friendly manner made him a friend to everyone and an inspiration to many.

On 9 December Geoffrey made a reconnaissance of the enemy's position in front of his own trenches. He crept forward slowly across the muddy, smashed landscape of no-man's-land, dodging the continual sweep of machine-gun fire until he was within a few yards of the enemy's lines. He brought back invaluable information as to the size and strength of the opposing forces and, as a result, became the recipient of a very special telegram of congratulation from his commanding officer. The day after (10 December), he was promoted to lieutenant. This young schoolboy was quickly building up a character of leadership and bravery.

Despite this, he longed to lead his men in a grand advance, and he didn't have to wait long. He was told he would be leading his men as part of the reinforcement troops in an attack on the enemy lines on 18 December. Zero hour for the main attack was pencilled in for 6 p.m. Three minutes before zero the first wave of attacking troops climbed up on to the parapet, wriggled through their defensive belts of barbed wire and lay down awaiting the whistle to advance together towards the German lines. In the noise of battle (the British artillery were laying down a fearsome barrage to keep the German soldiers out of their trenches) the whistle was not heard all along the line, and when the advance got going it was clear that the attacking line was not being maintained.

In his report after the event, Captain Loder wrote:

It was arranged that at 6pm the men should be posted over the parapet and to crawl out under the wire fence, and lie down. When this was done I was to blow my whistle and the line was then to move forward together, and walk as far as they could until the Germans opened fire and then push the front line trenches. Having reached the trench, I was to try and hold it if occupied, and if unoccupied to push on to the second line. The men carried spades and sandbags ... At about three minutes to 6pm the men were pushed over the parapet and lay down. I blew my whistle as loud as I could, but owing to the noise of the gun fire it appears it was not generally heard ... After advancing about 60 yds I could see that in several places the line was not being maintained, some men moving forward faster than others. I could see this by the flash of the guns. I collected the men nearest to me, and I found myself practically on the parapet before the Germans opened fire.

There was no wire entanglement at this point. We bayonetted and killed all the Germans we could see in the trench and then jumped down into it. There was a certain amount of shouting and confusion.

Although the central part of the attacking formation managed to enter and occupy the German trenches, the attack wasn't a raging success, and indeed in some areas, especially the right flank, it had failed completely. It was time to send in the reserves.

Second Lieutenant Ottley led his company from the front, over the parapet, through the defensive wire and across no-man's-land until they were in sight of the enemy lines. He raced to the German trench (there was no wire entanglement in his sector either), but as he reached the enemy lines he was hit and fell, mortally wounded, on the parapet of the German trenches. He was carried back to his own lines with great gallantry by Corporal Mitchell of the same corps, who insisted on helping him, despite being wounded himself and Lieutenant Ottley's repeated requests that he leave him alone in order to secure his own life. None of Ottley's men were able to occupy that trench.

Ottley was evacuated to the Australian hospital at Wimereux, where he died from his wounds on 21 December at 5 a.m., just a few short hours before the arrival of his parents. He was a month away from his 19th birthday. Posthumously, he was mentioned in Sir John French's dispatch of 14 January 1915 and was created a Companion of the Distinguished Service Order (*London Gazette*, 18 February 1915):

> For conspicuous gallantry in endeavouring to take a portion of the enemy's trenches after a previous effort had failed. In this attempt he was severely wounded and has since died.

His body was brought back to Scotland on Christmas Day and laid to rest at Lochaber, far away from the guns and the mayhem that had brought an untimely end to this brave young man. The train that carried the funeral party to Fort William was met at the station by a contingent of Argyll and Sutherland Highlanders, who carried the coffin draped in a Union Jack surmounted by sword and cap to the church of St Andrew. A pipe-and-drum band played 'Flowers of the Forest' as he was laid to rest. In memory of Lieutenant Geoffrey Claude Langdale Ottley there is a plaque situated within St Andrew's Episcopal church, High Street, Fort William.

9

GROUP CAPTAIN HUBERT WILLIAM GODFREY JONES MC

(4TH BATTALION, WELSH REGIMENT & RFC)

Hubert William Godfrey Jones was born in Llandudno, Wales, on 7 October 1890, the son of Thomas and Elizabeth Jones. He joined up with the 4th (Volunteer) Battalion, Welsh Regiment, obtaining a commission to second lieutenant in April 1913. When war was declared the following year this territorial battalion was quickly mobilised, moving from Carmarthen to Tunbridge Wells before moving up to the Forth and Tay defences in Scotland in early 1915. A few months later the battalion got the call and on 19 July they sailed as part of the 53rd (Welsh) Division from Devonport bound for Gallipoli, where they landed at Suvla Bay on 9 August.

Along with the rest of the division, Hubert was thrown straight into the fighting in and around Suvla in a desperate attempt to reignite the stuttering Allied advance. The next day the entire division was engaged in a large attack on Scimitar Hill, which was the culminating ridge of a spur running to the north-east of Chocolate Hill and the village of Anafarta Saghir.

The Turks were well prepared for this assault and although the attacking troops gained some ground the Turks launched repeated counter-attacks and a series of bush fires threatened to burn to death many of the soldiers, especially those that were wounded. The offensive was a disaster and ruined the division as an effective fighting force within forty-eight hours of its arrival in the area. The Imperial War Museum's history of Gallipoli records, '[It] was a terrible failure and was eventually abandoned having achieved nothing but a hefty casualty list and another division had been ruined during its first two days of action.'

Second Lieutenant Jones received gunshot wounds to both legs and his right hand during the bitter fighting at Scimitar Hill that day. The hot weather and lack of effective medical support at the time meant the wounds rapidly festered and became sceptic. His visit to the Gallipoli Peninsula was short-lived as he was quickly evacuated back to England to recover.

Once back in England, Jones transferred to the RFC and commenced his training to become a pilot. He finally gained his Royal Aero Club Aviators' Certificate (No. 2747) on 16 April 1916 while flying a Caudron biplane at Beatty Flying School, Hendon, and was officially seconded to the RFC on 22 July 1916. He was posted to No. 32 Squadron, RFC, flying Airco DH.2s that summer and was quickly involved in the action on the Somme. The squadron was under the command of Major Lionel W. Brabazon Rees, who had recently been awarded the VC for gallantry in dogfights over the Somme battlefield on 1 July 1916.

On 11 August, while flying an Airco DH.2 (7859), he recorded his first confirmed victory – an enemy Fokker E, which he engaged over Rancourt and forced out of control. It would be the first of seven confirmed victories during the war. He had to wait until 23 September for his second victory, however. He was once more patrolling over the Somme area in a DH.2 (A2533) when he engaged and destroyed an enemy LVG C two-seat reconnaissance biplane after emptying a drum of ammunition into the enemy aircraft from 50 yards' range.

Not satisfied with that victory, an hour later he was hot on the tail of another hostile plane, which he hit several times but could not confirm it was destroyed. The squadron combat report of the day takes up the story:

> On offensive patrol at about 3.40 p.m. pilot saw two hostile aircraft over Warlencourt at about 4,000 feet. He dived and engaged one from the rear and side at about 50 yards range. He fired nearly a drum, tracers hitting their mark when the hostile machines dived very steeply. He changed his drum but could not again see the hostile machines owing to the smoke from a large fire at Faucourt l'Abbaye. Lieutenant Wallace, who witnessed this, saw the hostile machine crash under the smoke pall, just north of Faucourt l'Abbaye, and as there was heavy shelling on the spot, the machine must have been blown to bits. The other hostile machine bolted.
>
> At 4.30 p.m. the pilot saw two hostile machines over Grevillers, at about 3,000 feet. He dived and engaged one, firing from the front and side, and then from the rear. Both times at about 50 yards range. The tracers were seen to hit their mark. Pilot was at 2,000 feet when he finished his drum. The hostile machine was diving and firing over his tail. Pilot lost sight of him when changing his drum. Lieutenant Henty witnessed this, and states that the hostile machine was certainly hit, and looked as if it was going to land east of Bapaume. He could not actually see him on the ground, owing to the bad visibility.

A week later, on 1 October, flying the same DH.2 (A2533) he claimed his third confirmed victim of the war, driving an enemy plane out of control over the Bihaucourt area. But his luck was about to run out in a big way. He became embroiled in a ferocious dogfight high above the Somme battlefields. The pilot he was jousting with enjoyed prodigious skill and dexterity and eventually shot Jones' plane to pieces, forcing it to crash to the ground. The plane plunged into a large shell hole, but amazingly he was able to crawl away from the wreckage largely unhurt. He had just become the thirtieth victim of the great German ace, Hauptmann Oswald Boelcke.

On 16 November 1916 he shared in two enemy aircraft being driven out of control over Loupart Wood, with Lieutenants M.J.J.G. Mare-Montembault and P.B.G. Hunt, while in the new year on 5 February he claimed an Albatross DI, out of control over Grevillers. On 15 February in the same sector of the front, he and two colleagues flew straight down the throat of an enemy formation consisting of ten machines. Undaunted and instead of doing the sensible thing and turning around, Jones led his men straight into the attack. Being so outnumbered, it is not surprising that his plane was hit and he was wounded.

Despite the wounds, he drove one of the hostile machines out of control. It was his seventh and final victory, and it would also earn him the Military Cross, the citation for which appeared in the *London Gazette* on 26 March 1917:

> Lieutenant (Temporary Captain) Hubert William Godfrey Jones, Welsh Regiment and R.F.C. For conspicuous gallantry in action. With a patrol of three scouts he attacked a hostile formation of ten enemy machines. Although wounded, he continued the combat and drove down an enemy machine. Later, although again wounded, he remained with his patrol until the enemy retired.

On 11 March 1917, he transferred to No. 24 Squadron, RFC, and was appointed flight commander. He continued to fly in front-line operations and was again wounded in combat over Roupy on 21 March. After a run-in with an enemy fighter his aircraft was badly shot up and was last seen spinning out of control at about 1,000ft above the ground. Once more he somehow survived the crash landing but he did sustain significant and painful injuries, as described in the proceedings of a subsequent Medical Board review and assessment of his condition:

> While flying over lines he was attacked by a German airplane and anti-aircraft guns. His plane was shot down and he sustained two wounds to his perineum, also extensive contusions to his back, chest and legs and left testicle from the fall … the wounds have healed, pains are much better, but the left testicle is somewhat atrophied.

This was effectively his final bow at the front line. After this incident his superiors decided to give him a rest from active duty and, once he had recovered sufficiently from his wounds, Jones was posted as an instructor to the CFS. During his time as an instructor he received both the Military Cross and also the Italian Silver Medal for Military Valour.

At the end of the war he was given command of No. 19 Squadron. Remaining a regular after the war, he again commanded No. 19 Squadron from July 1925 until August 1928, shortly before being placed on the retired list of officers. It was in 1928 that he changed his surname to Penderel.

Not wishing to lose the thrill of aviation, after the war he took part in numerous air races and exhibition flights during the 1920s and 1930s. He was good – so good that, like a golf professional, he was allotted a scratch handicap. One of his favourite races was the King's Cup Circuit of Britain, which he entered in 1924, 1925 and 1926. These races consisted of either one or two complete circuits of Britain, with the fastest lap times winning the race (with the handicap being taken into consideration). Jones always finished in the top four places and in 1926 won two prizes – third place overall and the fastest time to complete two laps of Britain (he completed the journey in a time of nine hours, forty-five minutes and fourteen seconds at an average speed of 151.9mph).

On 30 June 1934 in the Fifteenth Royal Air Force Display at RAF Hendon, Penderel represented RAF Fighting Area HQ and was one of ten competitors who took part in the 14-mile Headquarters race. *Flight International Magazine* of that day describes the scene:

> The scratch man, Wing Com. Penderel, Fighting Area, had already overtaken several others when he came round over the enclosures on the first lap, and from then on he could be seen overhauling other machines steadily. Due to the efficacy of the handicapping, Penderel finished outside the first three places.

Between January and March 1931 Squadron Leader Penderel commanded No. 216 Squadron's formation of three Vickers Victoria troop carriers on their 6,000-mile return flight from their base at Heliopolis, Cairo, to Capetown, where he was welcomed by the governor general, the Earl of Clarendon. For this flight he was awarded the Air Force Cross. He was invested at Buckingham Palace by King George V on 25 June 1931.

As well as flying, Penderel had a keen interest in geology, and between 1932 and 1933 he undertook a number of expeditions to explore Gulf Kebir and the desert interiors of Libya, looking for, among other things, the legendary lost oasis of Zerzura. One of his expeditions with Count Laszlo Almasy, a Hungarian desert researcher, loosely formed the basis for the book *The English Patient*.

After his expeditions, Penderel wrote a book covering his journeys and began to lecture at the Royal Geographical Society where he was admitted as a fellow. With another world war on the horizon, he was promoted to group captain in 1938 and in September 1939 became the first commander of No. 201 Group RAF, part of the General Reconnaissance Group, Middle East.

He was killed on 14 May 1943 while on a secret trial flight, piloting a Hurricane HV895 from RAF Middle Wallop over the Sudbourne battle-training area, when he crashed at Orford Ness. His ashes are interred at Llanguicke (St Ciwg) churchyard.

10

570618 CORPORAL FREDERICK GEORGE HEAD MM AND BAR

(17TH BATTALION, LONDON REGIMENT)

At his cremation in 1974, the local vicar described Frederick George Head as a 'lion and a lamb' – an apt description for many of the soldiers who fought in the First World War. Corporal Head's story was a common one for his era: attestation, training, sent to the front line, two and three-quarter years fighting the most dreadful war imaginable before a 'Blighty wound' took him back home to recover. Once in hospital he was left to convalesce and fight again, this time not a storm of steel, but a storm of emotion – loss and bereavement, anger, pride, guilt, relief and remorse. Trying to come to terms with what had gone before and what might come next.

In the summer of 1914, Frederick Head was happily going about his business as a bricklayer in London's East End. His life was about to change forever, however, when Great Britain declared war on Germany on 4 August. Head, along with a large number of his mates, downed tools and headed straight for their nearest army recruitment office. 'Kaiser Bill' had to be taught a lesson and the Germany Army needed to be kicked out of Belgium – fast. A trip to Tredegar Road was required to join the 5th London Brigade.

During the course of the next few months this band of volunteers became the 17th London Regiment, known to all as 'the Stepney and Poplar Rifles' or 'Pops'. Head and his mates had responded to Kitchener's call – the heady drug of patriotic fervour and foreign adventure became a potent force.

After training in the Home Counties, the Pops embarked for France in March 1915 as part of the 47th London Division. Landing at Le Havre, the battalion moved to Cassel. Later, there was a change of orders which sent the rest of the division to Allouagne. The battalion was moved to the new camp at Allouagne by a fleet of forty-two London buses driven by cockney drivers. The riflemen joked that these were the very same buses that they had ridden along the Mile End Road. After a period of further training and acclimatisation to conditions in the trenches, the battalion was ready to be moved up to the front and take their place in the front line. Many lambs on their way to the slaughter and many lions in the making.

Head and his mates were thrown into the mix almost immediately, tasting action at Givenchy during May. However, this was nothing compared to what lay around the corner. After a summer of being in the reserve line and being employed on various working parties up and down the line, the Pops were given orders to get ready to move out as the powers that be finalised the last pieces of what was to be the major Allied push in 1915 on the Western Front.

Hand-in-hand the British and French armies were organising themselves for a big push at Loos. It was meant to be the knockout blow that would send the enemy reeling backwards. However, not for the first or the last time, the grandiose promises of the army hierarchy fell flat. The end result for the Pops and many other regiments of Lord Kitchener's New

Armies was a huge amount of bloodletting. During bitter fighting at Loos between 25 and 28 September the Pops suffered 124 casualties either killed, missing or wounded. Indeed, the Pops got off relatively lightly compared to many – all in all, the Allies took a hammering with a dreadful tally of 61,000 killed, missing or wounded in just four days.

Amidst all this, Head was already beginning to emerge as one of the battalion characters and his friends were starting to celebrate his bravery in the face of the enemy. In his role as runner, Head was well known and well respected by the whole battalion. In a time when wireless and telephone communications were far from reliable, runners were used to send orders to the front and to send messages back to HQ from forward positions. It was a hair-raising and dangerous job as, more often than not, it involved passing over ground that was swept by enemy fire.

One of his best friends, Will Smith, wrote home endearingly of him to another pal back in England, 'Pluck! My word, he's small but as brave as any London man can be. I remember him at Loos walking along with messages, smoking a pipe as if the world's trouble were nothing to him.' Later, in the same letter, his friend recounted an episode of almost suicidal courage:

> Freddy has been mentioned in despatches three times. Once, a shell burst through the roof of the signaller's dugout and did not explode. It was a good size one too. Freddy did not run. He just picked it up and put it over the top out of harm's way, a deed that it takes a British soldier to do. There is no thinking twice with him.

Head's first winter in the trenches was pretty miserable. November and December 1915 were wet and cold, and life was carved up between consolidating existing positions and light training well back from the front line. In the spring of 1916 things warmed up a bit, in more ways than one, as suddenly Head found himself in the thick of it at Vimy Ridge. Sandwiched into the narrow dip between the German front line and their own HQ behind them, Head and the rest of the Pops were being pounded relentlessly by enemy artillery fire and communication was completely lost. Divisional HQ was at a loss to know whether to reinforce or withdraw. Confusion reigned.

Later, in hospital, Head recounted the story in the infirmary's own publication, *The Stebonheath Journal*:

> During our tour in the trenches at Vimy Ridge the Bosche exploded a mine on our front, and at about the same moment opened out a terrific bombardment. All wires were smashed and the officers at Headquarters were unable to get any news as to what happened. Thinking that the Bosche had captured our front line the Officer Commanding came and asked for two volunteers to go forward and find out what was happening. I said that I would go, providing I went alone, as it would be hard luck to have two men knocked out where one man might do it. It was then arranged that if I did not return within half an hour another would be sent.
>
> I reached our front line (but how I cannot explain), and found our men still held on, and that the mine had fallen short. I obtained all the information necessary, and got back quite safe and reported to HQ. I was then asked to guide a Bombing section with bombs up to our right and again succeeded and returned safely. I was recommended, and in June 1916 received the news that I had been awarded the Military Medal.

Corporal Head received his medal ribbon from the major general while the battalion was in reserve, during the afternoon of 19 June 1916. The news of the award of the medal was published in the *London Gazette* in August and in the *East End News* in September. In between times, friends both at the front and back home toasted Head. He received many letters of congratulations. Among them was one from his old headmaster, Thomas Rand of Marner Street School in Bromley-by-Bow:

My dear Head,

On behalf of the whole school (boys and teachers) allow me to congratulate you most heartily on having the MM [Military Medal].

We gave three Marner whispers (if you don't know what they are ask Smiffee) when the news was read to the whole school assembled in the hall and we are reserving a shout for you when you get back. So mind you come and take it.

I have heard that two other Marner boys have gained distinctions and you will hear about them if they are confirmed on enquiry from Webzell later on.

We have on roll 450 odd names and I know, everyone, dares to do his level best for his regiment or ship when the call comes.

The old school is proud of every one of you. God bless you all! With our heartiest congratulations and best of good wishes.

Yours faithfully,

Thos. R. Rand

For the British, the summer of 1916 exploded into action with the Battle of the Somme on 1 July, a battle that continued on and on towards early autumn. During some particularly savage fighting north-east of Albert, an early opportunity to capture a commanding ridge looking down across the back positions of the Hindenburg Line had been wasted. Having driven the Germans out of High Wood, on the crest of this ridge, deliberation and confusion had allowed the enemy to re-infiltrate the thick undergrowth and stay in control of this vital strategic point.

After weeks of skirmishing, the thick woods and lush farmland surrounding it had been completely obliterated. So much so that the area was unrecognisable and only smoking stumps remained where High Wood had once stood. Early in September the Pops were in training to take the strongpoint. Head and his friends were girding themselves for something they knew might take many of their lives. In a local *estaminet* (café) behind the lines, they got themselves totally drunk the night before being sent up the line ready for one last bash at taking the wood and driving on to take the prize of Bapaume before winter set in.

A bloody conflict was expected by all, but confidence was high. The British Army had a new secret weapon. Despite reservations by the 47th divisional commander, Major General Barter, four tanks were to be ordered into and around what was left of High Wood to assist the infantry in its bid to break through the German line. To precede the proposed attack, a three-day artillery bombardment was put in place along the entire attacking front. Everywhere, that is, except High Wood. The powers that be thought the opposing trench lines were too close to each other for such a bombardment to be carried out safely, and also this area was to have the new superweapon – the tank – so it wouldn't be too much of a problem not to have artillery back up. Head recounts seeing this new weapon in action (or rather inaction, as predicted failure among the smashed tree stumps proved well founded) in a later letter. He was not impressed, 'The tank which should have smashed our wire broke down before it.' The failure of the tanks left Head and his mates at the mercy of the omnipotent German machine guns: 'The barbed wire not being smashed the boys were held up and were absolutely slaughtered for about two hours by machine gun, rifle fire and artillery.'

Zero hour was set for 6.20 a.m. However, no one told the 15th Londons (Civil Service Rifles), who were positioned to the right of the Pops and were convinced that zero was in fact 5.50 a.m. As the hands of their watches reached this earlier time the officers and men of the 15th clambered out of their trenches and charged forward towards the enemy lines to the amazement of the Pops, who remained where they were. Then, fifteen minutes later, they saw a sight that would remain with them for the rest of their days. An iron monster rumbled towards them, across the abandoned trench and followed the 15th Londons into the battle. It was a tank named Delilah. It was the first tank any of the soldiers had ever seen.

All of this activity had, of course, alerted the Germans that something heavy was about to hit them. When the Pops, along with their neighbours on the left, the 18th London Regiment (Irish Rifles), climbed out of their trenches at 6.20 a.m. – the correct time for the attack – the defenders were ready and waiting for them. The attacking Londoners were welcomed by a hail of machine-gun and rifle fire:

At 6.20am our artillery bombardment (which had been going on steadily since 17th) became intense; and the Btn launched an attack in 4 waves of companies on a platoon frontage, with [the] object of taking 1st two lines of trenches and constructing a strong point for 1 platoon and 2 Vickers guns.

Enemy met attack with very heavy machine gun fire and attack was held up for nearly 3 hours. Later a fresh assault was made and all Btn objectives occupied about 10.30am.

By 1 p.m. the next day, through the sheer willpower and doggedness of the men on the ground, High Wood was finally taken and within a week the Germans had been pushed as far back as Eaucourt L'Abbaye in this sector. Any further efforts at driving on towards Bapaume, however, were scotched by a particularly resilient defence from the enemy and heavy autumn rain.

In their bid for High Wood, casualties for the Pops had been very high: 332 killed, missing or wounded. Among the dead was Head's pal, Harry Litchfield. The night of their drinking spree, Harry had kept everyone waiting while he sewed on his brand-new corporal stripes. While digging out the dead at a bombed mortar base, Head had come across Harry, at first only identifying him by his new stripes on an arm protruding from the mud:

> I did not have to dig long when I saw that it was Harry Litchfield's face, all muddy, that I came to. I could not stay and dig him right up but I got to his tunic pocket and took his papers out of his pay book. There was nothing of any use there so I destroyed the papers and handed his pay book into HQ and reported him killed. I am not certain but I think it was the next morning when I saw them carrying Tom Harvey down on a stretcher. I gave them a little hand with him across a few trenches and shook hands with him before they took him right away.

By early October both sides were establishing new lines and beginning to think about settling down for the winter.

Winter 1916 for the Pops was spent in Flanders. In the spring they were moved into the line near Messines, just south of the Commes Canal. After the detonation of the mines there, the 47th Division as a whole successfully completed their objectives, with Head's team of runners coming in for particular praise in the divisional history.

In June 1917 the whole division was moved back to a restful area well away from the front after being bogged down in the mud for the previous nine months. August 1917 brought a move to the town of Ypres itself in readiness to take up positions around the Roulers railway. Heavy summer rain in this low-lying, already battered area of the front line made conditions horrendous. At such a time the role of the runners became even more essential than normal. Trenches were full of water and liquid mud, and laying cables for phone lines was impossible.

By mid-September, Head found himself in the line at Bellewarde Ridge, just north of Menin Road, preparing the trenches for the major offensive the following week. During this time night raids continued and general skirmishing took place. While assisting stretcher bearers in carrying wounded back to forward medical posts, a trench mortar base nearby was shelled. With artillery fire falling all around, Head went out on his own, shovel in hand, to see what he could do:

[That night] we were being shelled heavily and I was ordered to the left post of our battalion with a stretcher, and just previous to it getting dark I was ready to make a start on my journey when a chap came rushing up and said that a trench mortar position had been blown up and all the team buried. I found a shovel and rushed to where I knew there was a trench mortar position. When I arrived the first thing I saw was the Sergeant in charge of the team buried up to his neck in a small dug-out with a plank holding the earth above his head from falling on him. He was shouting for me to get him out first, but I could hear groans coming from the earth nearer to me, so I told the Sergeant to hang on, as he was able to breathe, while I dug for the chap I could hear groaning. It was hard work digging with the shovel, as I did not know if I was getting towards his head or his feet and was afraid of sticking the shovel into him. I got him out after a short struggle, and he was properly shaken up and could not stand. I left him lying where he was while I got the Sergeant out and then carried him to our Headquarters from where he was taken to our regimental aid post. There were no others of the team buried there, so I presumed they had hopped it when they saw the shell explode in their post. I was then recommended and heard that I had been awarded the Bar [to the Military Medal] in October 1917.

Once again Head's bravery had been rightly rewarded.

As the main offensive began, Head and the rest of the Pops were moved south to a quieter sector near Bourlon Wood. The quietness did not last long, however, and they were pressed once more into action in late November to take Bourlon Wood itself. A German attack led to frighteningly heavy casualties, and among them this time was Head. On 30 November 1917, while in the front line with his commanding officer and adjutant, he fell victim to chlorine gas and was almost completely overcome. Unable to see and with breathing difficulties, Head was helped back from the line by the two officers in order to receive treatment. Having rested, and thinking he would recover quickly, he realised he could not go on and reluctantly decided to let himself be helped back to receive more lengthy medical care.

Writing after the war, Field Marshal Haig said this of the situation at Bourlon Wood on 30 November:

[The German attack] began with a very heavy bombardment of the kind that everybody had now come to expect. Germany still had a monopoly of mustard gas and great stocks of it. Saturation by this weapon seemed, reasonably enough, to be the best way in which to make the English divisions ready to receive their assailants. Choked for a certainty; with luck, blinded also. It worked quite well. German shells doused the wood with dichloroethyl sulphate, known since 1854 but its potentialities only recently appreciated by the Teutonic mind, and poisoned the undergrowth. On the right was 1/19th London Regiment, still better known as the Popular and Stepney Rifles, commanded by Lt Col R S I Friend of the Buffs. When the gas shells began to fall it [19th] counted some 600 effectives. By the time the gassing was over about 70 were on their feet. The rest were blinded. All this did little for the Kaiser's regiments. The guns, rifles and machine-guns of London tore into the attackers ...

Although Haig makes a mistake in this passage – the 1/19th were in fact the St Pancras Rifles, although the Pops were on the right and the 1/19th were on the left – the casualty numbers were similar in both battalions. The Pops were also decimated by gas on this day.

Corporal Head struggled to recover sufficiently from his gassing to be allowed to return to the front, and by the middle of December he was back in the UK convalescing at Stebonheath Hospital, Llanelli, South Wales. He was released from hospital in February 1918 but he was not able to re-join his mates at the front line. He would see out the war in England, engaged in training duties. This particular lion had done his duty.

11

2732 PRIVATE JOHN EVELYN CARR

(1ST BATTALION, LONDON SCOTTISH)

John Evelyn Carr was 43 years old when war was declared in the summer of 1914. Although he was the managing director of Scremerston Coal Company near Berwick-upon-Tweed, he travelled down to London to sign up for military service as soon as Great Britain had sounded the bugle in August 1914. He was desperate to join up and knocked ten years off his age to ensure he was able to meet the age requirements for military service. He enlisted as Private No. 2732 in the 1st Battalion, London Scottish. His life was about to change dramatically.

Carr was born into a successful and prominent local family in Gosforth, Newcastle upon Tyne, on 21 February 1871. He was one of fourteen children and was educated at Durham School, the local public school. John Evelyn's father, John Carr, was a successful entrepreneur and businessman, trying his hand as a colliery owner, timber merchant, coal exporter, banker with the Newcastle and District Bank, and a director of the Blyth and Tyne Railway. He was also a prominent member of the Gosforth Parish church, where he served as the vicar's warden.

However, disaster struck when the Newcastle and District Bank suffered severe losses. As a result, the proprietors were forced to sell their assets to save the bank. In 1892 the sale of most of the family colliery interests, the shareholding in the Tyne and Blyth Railway and even the family home, Roseworth House, took place. The family were forced to move out of the area and re-establish themselves at Sea House, a large residence on the coast near Berwick-upon-Tweed.

John Carr senior died two years later in 1894, leaving John Evelyn, at the age of 23, to take on more of the family and business responsibilities. He rose to the challenge very well and as the years passed Carr established himself in northeast society, working his way up to become the managing director of Scremerston Coal Company and a member of Northumberland County Council. He was also a member of the Berwick-upon-Tweed Harbour Commission, and held a commission in the Northumberland Artillery Volunteers. Outside of work he played rugby for Northumberland County, as well as pursuing more genteel activities such as fishing, hunting and shooting. He married Gertrude Isabella Moncrieff in 1900.

Everything seemed to be going swimmingly for Carr, both his family life and business were doing great. Then Germany declared war. As a man of a certain socio-economic standing, it is perhaps unusual that Carr signed up as a lowly private soldier. However, the London Scottish was a remarkable territorial regiment. Unlike the regular units of the pre-war British Army, where the majority of ordinary soldiers joined up to escape poverty, prison or both, the ranks of the London Scottish were composed of men of a higher social standing. Carr's battalion, the 1st, contained merchants, engineers, farmers, surveyors, solicitors, doctors,

barristers, artists and musicians. There were also many men
of education in the ranks, as well as clerks from banks,
underwriters and stockbrokers. It was a rule of the regiment
that no man could hold a commission unless he had served
in the ranks as an ordinary soldier.

After signing on the dotted line in London, Carr had less
than a month of training before he found himself on board
the SS *Winifredian* at Southampton. The voyage to France
began after dark on 15 September 1914, eventually docking
at Le Havre on 16 September. When they disembarked the
regimental pipers played the 'Marseillaise' and they marched
through the streets of the town; streets that were lined with
large cheering crowds welcoming the British liberators. In a
blink of an eye, John Evelyn Carr had transformed himself
from quiet, successful businessman to a soldier of war.

With all the emotion and energy of those early days in
September 1914, the soldiers of the London Scottish were
disappointed that they were not needed to go straight into
the thick of the fighting. Instead of being allowed to give
the Bosch a bit of a kicking, they had to accept rather less
glamourous duties; for the next five weeks, Carr and his new
mates were employed up and down northern France working on installing and improving logistic and communications
lines for the BEF. The work was hard, tiring and immensely
unimaginative, and many of the soldiers, Carr included, were
starting to wonder if they would ever get to see a German
soldier for real.

In early October, though, the pace of things picked
up. Germany captured Antwerp and began to pour into
Belgium and bear down on France. The first detachment
of the BEF arrived in Ypres just in time to plug the gap
between the French and Belgian armies, but they were
outnumbered and, once the First Battle of Ypres began on

20 October, it was only a matter of time before the thin British line would be overrun. On 25 October the call went out for every available regiment to move to the area to help stem the tide.

Carr was in Nantes when the call went out for the London Scottish to get a taste of life in the front line. Despite the fact that they had not had any meaningful training while in France, and many of the men had never even practised firing their new rifles, they were to be thrown into the battle along the Messines Ridge to support the beleaguered BEF, who were struggling to stop the German advance.

The first wave of London Scottish arrived in Ypres on 30 October, and received orders the next day to move up to the Messines–Wytschaete Ridge to fill a dangerous gap in the line and help out the carabiniers, who were already on the ridge and having a rough time of it. As they moved up the slope of the ridge the London Scottish came under heavy rifle fire, the men carried out the advance at a steady pace reminiscent of pre-war practice, but as they reached the crest the enemy fire was so intense that they had no choice but to find cover, dig in as best they could, sit tight and wait for the enemy counter-attack that was bound to appear.

It came at around 9 p.m. Against the massed German attacks these raw recruits gave a good account of themselves. They couldn't match the fifteen rounds a minute rapid rifle fire of the regulars, but they stood their ground and inflicted heavy casualties upon their attackers. They were not helped by their new hardware; often their rifles would jam or the magazine spring was too weak, and the London Scottish were sometimes reduced to loading and firing just single shots. Despite this inconvenience, wave after wave of attacks were deflected until, at 2 a.m., the Germans finally managed to drive through the British lines.

As the waves of attacking soldiers poured into the trenches all along the front they quickly threatened to completely surround the London Scottish, who had just realised that they had been brought up to the lines with no maps and no real knowledge of the terrain. Although many were wounded and all of them were exhausted, the officers rallied the men and, using the moon and a good deal of guesswork, quickly worked out a way of extricating themselves from their present predicament. Fortunately the Germans were tired too and didn't press home their advantage as hard as they perhaps could have, and this respite provided the London Scottish with the lull they needed to get out of there. The regimental roll call twenty-four hours later revealed 394 casualties killed, wounded or missing.

Fortunately for Carr, his trek over from Nantes had meant that he didn't join the rest of the battalion until after the Battle of Messines had finished, but he didn't have long to wait to get a taste of front-line action himself. On 5 November they received orders to join up with the 4th Guards Brigade in the woods near Klein Zillebeke where, on 8 November, they took over the defence of a line in what was then known as Brown Road Wood. There were no trenches to speak of, just a line of random holes in the ground; some were joined up, others weren't.

Due to the beating they had taken at Messines and the fact that they still hadn't received new rifles to replace their defective ones, the London Scottish could only offer a feeble defensive line. But they were there and ready for anything the Germans could throw at them. Almost as soon as they were in position the enemy started to throw 'lots' at them – lots of shells. For six days non-stop German shells rained down on the thinly defended lines. For Carr and the rest of the battalion this was a thoroughly miserable time. They had no effective cover and had to cope with falling trees and exploding showers of splinters and other foliage as well as the enemy artillery. It was almost impossible to bring up food and supplies to the front line as shattered trees blocked every inch of the wood. In his diary, Carr noted the 'fearful' devastation, cottages and houses in ruins, dead horses, pigs, cattle and poultry strewn all over the place, as well as roads broken up by shelling and broken trees.

During the heavy shelling Private Carr was knocked unconscious by a shrapnel blow to the back of the neck. He recovered and continued to fight until one of the fingers on his right hand was hit by another shell splinter, which made it impossible for him to reload and fire his rifle. He was evacuated to the rear for his wounds to be evaluated and dressed. His hand was bad enough for him to be shipped off back to England for recovery. He ended up at Cottesbrook Military Hospital in Northamptonshire to recover from his wounds and later returned to Scremerston on leave to see his wife.

Meanwhile, back in Brown Road Wood, the big German offensive that everyone expected finally took place on 11 November, but it was checked by a fanatical defence and a deluge of rain which reduced the intensity of any subsequent attacks. The war diary of the battalion had this to say of their time in the woods: 'From Nov 8th to 13th we were constantly, heavily shelled and attacked in varying degrees by night and day, the position was one of continual anxiety ...' Despite the anxiety, the line held. But at a cost – when they were finally relieved at 11 p.m. on 13 November, only 280 soldiers of an already beleaguered battalion were left.

Back in England, Carr continued his recuperation. When he was fully recovered he was granted a commission as a lieutenant on the general list of the territorial reserve with effect from 10 April 1915, in the 8th Battalion, Manchester

Regiment, which he joined at Cavendish Dock Airship Shed, Barrow. However, the last thing he wanted to do was spend the rest of the war guarding airship sheds in England. He was itching to get back to France and, despite his age, wounds and experiences at the front line, wanted a transfer to a front-line regiment. His wish was granted when he managed to obtain a transfer to a new battalion that was being formed on the back of Lord Kitchener's Call to Arms. He joined the 11th (Service) Battalion, Sherwood Foresters at Martinique Barracks, Bordon, in Hampshire on 8 August 1915 and was reappointed to a temporary commission as a lieutenant. On 20 August 1915 the battalion was ordered to France – Carr was going back to war.

By the time Carr reported for duty at No. 36 Casualty Clearing Station (CCS), just east of Albert, the preliminary bombardment prior to the Battle of the Somme was well under way, smashing the German lines to pieces. It was 27 June 1916. His battalion, 11th Sherwood Foresters, was preparing for their role in the attack, and it is likely his true age had been discovered. This, along with his earlier wounding, prevented him from going back to front-line duty:

A car was ordered to take me to the 36th Casualty Clearing Station (CCS) at 5.00pm. I reported to OC [officer commanding] Colonel Thompson who told me my job would be to take charge of fifty men, stretcher-bearers, and to entrain the wounded, supervise the burying of dead German prisoners etc. There are about 18 of us in the mess, mostly MOs [medical officers]. At 11.00pm heavy firing was proceeding and the sky was almost continually lit up by gun flashes and shells bursting. I started my duties this morning.

Carr noted on 28 June:

When wounded men arrive I meet them and send all the stretcher cases that require immediate operation to a large ward prepared for them, and the walking wounded and more slight cases to a large tent. After they have been attended to and their wounds dressed I collect first the stretcher cases and have them conveyed to the train, which I have to have in readiness and have them put on board, and then collect the 'walkers' and get them on board, getting receipts from the OC of train. I appear to have a good lot of men, mostly regular soldiers and some good sergeants. They mostly consist of those who have been wounded themselves at the very beginning of the war, and they are a pretty tough lot.

Meanwhile, the preparations for the 'big push' of 1916 were almost reaching their peak. It was 30 June, the day before the battle, and Carr seemed to have a premonition of what the next twenty-four hours would hold, as he wrote:

… went up the hill after tea to watch the bombardment The infantry are to go over about 7.30 tomorrow morning. Most of the reserves are beginning to move up from here tonight. It gives you a lump in the throat to see the reinforcements going up singing as happy and splendid as possible.

The following day threatened to be quite busy for the men and nurses of the 36th CCS – and it didn't disappoint:

At 6.30am I went up on the hill behind Albert and saw our artillery pounding the Hun trenches to pieces. Then there was a lull and we knew that the infantry were advancing. I waited until 8.00am and then rushed down, as I knew what work would be before me. I spent, I think, the worst day of my life. The wounded began pouring in about 11.00am and continued coming all day.

In the two stations we had almost 4,000 cases. I evacuated two trains including 966 cases, many being terribly mutilated. The sights and agonies of the men are too awful for words.

I saw many of the officers and men I knew, and heard bits of the fight from them. It is a sight never to be forgotten – seeing these splendid men lying like helpless babies. I have 500 sitting cases to get away from No. 36 tomorrow morning at 1.30, so I am going down for an hour.

A lovely summer day and one I shall never forget. My battalion (as good as any in the British Army) was almost entirely demolished. Many of my best pals were killed. The whole of our Brigade [70th] which went over at La Boisselle was almost wiped out.

Carr's battalion, 11th Sherwood Foresters, took heavy casualties when moving forward to the British front line from reserve at Authuille Wood. In their attack on Ovillers–La Boisselle they advanced to the German front line, but machine-gun fire from the front and both flanks stopped their attack. They were relieved at night and withdrew to Long Valley. Their total casualties on that single day were 518.

On the evening of 1 July and during the night, CCSs became acutely congested because of the unexpectedly high casualty rate. The efficiency of the field ambulances in delivering casualties to CCSs was not matched by the ambulance trains, which failed to get to CCSs in sufficient numbers to evacuate them. To assist in this crisis, two additional surgical teams and fifty stretcher bearers from the Royal Army Medical Corps (RAMC) were sent to No. 36 CCS.

Such were the losses that, on 16 July 1916, Carr was ordered to return to what remained of the 11th Sherwood Foresters, where his experience would enable him to assist in building up the battalion from the cadre left behind for this purpose and with the training of reinforcements.

In 1917 Carr went to Italy with the 11th Sherwoods, and served with them at the front until the end of the war. He held a special staff appointment from September 1918 until April 1919, and was adjutant of the Labour Corps until he relinquished his commission on completing his service on 14 November 1919, fully one year after the signing of the Armistice.

Military life obviously suited him, as he did not show any willingness to return home quickly after the end of the war. He had been mentioned in dispatches three times and he was rightly proud of the part he played in these monumental events. On demobilisation he was allowed to keep the rank of captain, and back in civilian life no one referred to him as 'Mr Carr', it was always 'Captain Carr'. He was known later as a modest, kind gentleman with a tough, formidable streak. No doubt he had been hardened by the five years of war and suffering he had both witnessed and endured.

On his eventual return Carr threw himself back into his businesses. Although he could never match his father's wealth and success, he did well as a small businessman. He built numerous houses in his local area and a garage and petrol station along the A1. He also ran sand and gravel works and supplied local builders with concrete blocks and slabs. He kept up his association with the London Scottish throughout the rest of his life, attending dinners and functions as and when he could. His last appearance was a dinner at the Regimental Headquarters, 59 Buckingham Gate, in 1956.

John Evelyn Carr died on 6 February 1958, just a few weeks shy of his 88th birthday.

12

BRIGADIER BASIL BEDSMORE RACKHAM CBE, MC AND BAR

(HAWKE BATTALION, ROYAL NAVAL DIVISION)

Basil Bedsmore Rackham was born into a traditional miller's family at Wickham Market, Suffolk on 20 November 1896. The Rackham family were steeped in old-time Suffolk and yeoman tradition. Basil's father, Reuben, was a man of the earth, owning a farm as well as a water mill at Wickham Market. Basil's mother originally came from Staffordshire, her father being the long-time organist at Lichfield Cathedral.

Basil had two brothers and two sisters, and of the brothers he was the youngest by a couple of years. The Great War would bestow favourable fortunes upon the young males of the Rackham family. Basil's eldest brother, Edward, didn't see active service because he stayed to work in the mill as, by the time war broke out, Reuben was getting on in years and was starting to struggle with the running of the mill on his own. Edward was seen as an essential part of the war work-force and placed in the army reserve, though he was never called up for action. Basil would turn out to have a glittering military career, both in the First World War and beyond, while the middle son, Robert, was commissioned into the Royal Marines and also survived the war.

When the dominating powers of Europe locked horns in the summer of 1914, the young Basil had only one thought – to join up as soon as he could and do his bit for king and country. As he was only 17, he gravitated towards the navy, rather than the army, purely due to the lower age limit imposed at that time by the navy (17 as opposed to 18 for the army). The Royal Naval Division (RND) were on a big recruitment drive as they were in desperate need of new recruits for three of its battalions – Hawke, Benbow and Collingwood – which had practically ceased to exist after their recent expedition to Antwerp during October 1914.

As part of this recruitment drive, the RND had started the formation of a public schools unit and, with a public school upbringing and two years in the Officer Training Corps, this appealed to the young Basil Rackham. So, on 8 January 1915 Basil, along with his brother Robert, joined up at the Union Jack Club, just outside London Waterloo station. As he signed up and was placed on the nominal roll of the Public Schools Battalion, RND, he was of the opinion, like many young men of the time, that he was about to embark on a great adventure that would be over in a few months. He genuinely expected to be back in Wickham Market in time to open his Christmas presents.

At the Union Jack Club he was duly vaccinated, given ten days' leave and instructed to rejoin at HMS *Victory*, a training barracks for the RND, at the end of his leave. Immediately upon his return there was an outbreak of spotted fever. Rackham was one of those with symptoms and was immediately quarantined while the rest of his battalion went to Blandford for further training. In the end, though, he was informed he had measles, not spotted fever.

In reality the public schools battalion didn't materialise, as the powers that be in the RND thought it was a waste of talent having all these highly educated young men in the rank and file. Therefore, many of them were split up to serve as officers in other battalions.

At 3.30 a.m. on Sunday, 9 May 1915, while Rackham was still convalescing from measles, the RND set sail for the Dardanelles without him. While his new-found friends dug themselves in along rocky terrain and prepared to fight the Turks, Rackham slowly recovered from his illness and followed in the footsteps of his original battalion as he travelled down to Blandford to resume his own training. On 12 July 1915, Rackham was appointed to a commission as temporary sub lieutenant.

The training he underwent was not typical naval training; it was trench warfare, small-arms training and digging – lots of digging. It was more akin to army infantry training than anything even remotely naval. It was, in fact, training for Gallipoli, as Rackham and the rest of the men at Blandford were earmarked to move out to the peninsula as a second-wave reinforcement to back up the RND battalions that had already moved out there. Throughout the duration of training, wounded officers from the first wave returned to England and were able to give valuable information as to the terrain, the conditions and details of those military tactics that had worked and those that hadn't. As the training continued, news filtered through to the officers and men stationed at Blandford about the current fighting on the peninsula and the mauling that their comrades in the RND had taken in the ensuing battles. They were desperate to get out there and help their mates. And they would get their chance soon enough …

On 8 October 1915, Rackham was given a few days' leave. When he returned to base on 14 October it was time to get ready for war. After a hectic time trying to organise men, supplies, transportation, rations and everything else needed for the campaign, Rackham and the rest of the men finally entrained at Blandford, heading towards Southampton. They were given a great send-off from a very energetic and enthusiastic crowd, waving flags and cheering the train full of men on their way towards their greatest adventure.

However, they were soon in Southampton, where the atmosphere was very different. No crowds, no cheering – nothing. They went straight to the docks and boarded their ship. They had a job to do.

As an officer, Sub Lieutenant Rackham had fairly comfortable accommodation on board the troopship (unlike the crowded ratings) and food and general conditions were, on the whole, very good. On the way to the peninsula they stopped briefly at Malta. Officers were allowed ashore, ratings were not. Rackham and a number of the officers took the opportunity to get off the ship and have a walk. Although only there for a day he managed to have a good look around the shops and visit some of his wounded RND colleagues at the local military hospitals.

From Malta, the next stop on the journey was the town of Mudros, on the Greek island of Lemnos. Mudros was a very busy harbour town and at this time would have been a remarkable sight with all the naval military activity in the vicinity. When Rackham entered the harbour it was even more crowded than usual, as there were three very large liners in the harbour, among all the other cruisers and assorted military vessels, two of which were the *Equitania*, a converted hospital ship, and RMS *Olympic*, the sister ship of the famous *Titanic*. It was indeed a most impressive sight.

Once they found a place to weigh anchor, the ratings and the officers went ashore and made their home in a tented camp for a couple of days in final preparation for the last part of the voyage and the landings on the beaches. Conditions were terrible; it was very hot and there were too many people for the camp to cope with. Rations were limited and the tents and other amenities were cramped and basic, even for the officers.

It was with a collective sigh of relief that, a few days later, they were all back on board a smaller boat and heading straight for the peninsula. The final leg of the journey was uneventful and soon they landed on V Beach, Cape Helles, the scene of chaos and death just a few months earlier when the first Allied landings struggled ashore in the face of severe Turkish machine-gun fire.

This time, the men who clambered ashore that night were completely unmolested. The SS *River Clyde* landing boat was still *in situ* and this vessel was once more used to disembark troops and materials directly on to the beach. There was absolutely no opposition and Rackham, by now attached to D Company, Hawke Battalion, RND, and the rest of the new arrivals were met by fellow Hawke Battalion officers who had been stationed on the peninsula since May. They were taken swiftly up to their camp, situated at Backhouse Post, marked by a biscuit tin (now on display in the Museum of the Royal Scots), which was a reserve position about 3 miles from the front line. Once there, they tried to get comfortable.

By this time in the proceedings the general fighting on the peninsula had settled down somewhat, being made up of numerous localised, small-scale attacks and raids, rather than great ranging offensives across an elongated front line. Rackham was the youngest officer in the battalion and was nicknamed 'Baby Rackham'. He commanded a platoon made up of five petty officers and twenty-five ratings. Life in the trenches was particularly tedious, uncomfortable and fraught with danger, and during the hours of sunlight the troops were not able to move around too much as any kind of significant movement would instantly attract shell fire. Every metre of the peninsula was in the shadow of enemy artillery, so they did what they could to improve the trenches without attracting the wrath of the Turkish guns. During those first weeks in the trenches, part of Rackham was envious of his fellow naval colleagues who were actually fighting a war at sea, rather than living in the trenches. However, those sailors had their own demons to deal with in the shape of U-boats and hidden mine belts – it was not all fun and games on board ship either.

One advantage of being on board ship was that sailors didn't have to deal with the flies. Although still a teenager, Rackham quickly became inured to the death and futility of war. He just accepted that he was at war and got on with it – apart from the flies. The flies were something he could never get used to. Every time he opened a tin of bully beef or a jar of jam, it was immediately swarmed with flies. By the time he had a piece of food on his fork and towards his mouth that piece of food was also covered in flies. With the heat, the flies and the close proximity of dead bodies (both Allied and Turkish), the smell that hung over the battlefield was considerable.

The combined effects of these elements were pushed to the fore of Rackham's consciousness during the final days of 1915. A couple of days before Christmas, the Turks let loose a very heavy bombardment on the lines held by the Hawke Battalion which lasted for three days. In those three days the battalion lost around seventy men, killed or wounded. In the thick of the shelling, Rackham complained to his company commander of a 'deluge of spare parts' that had been thrown up and sprayed among his platoon by the fierce bombard-ment. To be fair to Rackham, he had a point – the 'spare parts' in question were random pieces of Turkish arms and legs that had been buried for a while until the guns had thrown them from their resting place. Suffice to say that these limbs and body parts were past their best and to be bombarded with such missiles, as well as those of a more explosive nature, was far from fun for Rackham and his group of men.

By now the weather had turned and the general temperatures had dropped significantly, especially at night when it would get very cold. Warm clothing was in short supply and severe blizzards rendered the trenches knee-deep in water. Life was very miserable, especially in the front line where hot food was in short supply, apart from the odd brew of tea during the night. There were very few creature comforts even for officers and the one saving grace was the naval rum ration which, larger than the normal army ration, was dished out every day where possible.

During a quiet period when his platoon was positioned in reserve, Rackham and a few other officers made an unofficial visit to the ANZAC (Australian and New Zealand Army Corps) area. The ANZACs had already moved out and all was quiet. He was appalled at the overall conditions that the soldiers had been asked to live and fight in. The terrain was terrible, very rough and rocky, and as a consequence it was impossible to construct continuous safe lines of trenches. Also, the position of the lines and dugouts were less strategic and more often located where they were physically able to dig.

On 29 December the Hawke Battalion left the front-line trenches for the last time. As they settled down in reserve, all energies and resources were funnelled into organising the evacuation. It was the role of the Hawke Battalion to provide the garrison of the front line for the entire divisional front while the bulk of the men and supplies were evacuated, they would then drop back to defend the reserve lines until the final hours when they would be allowed to board the ships and get off the island. Just forty-eight hours before 'Y' night of the evacuation, the enemy sent over observer planes which flew low over the Allied lines. The spotters couldn't have failed to see the lack of guns, and Rackham and his men, huddled down in the trenches, felt very exposed.

If they had felt the need, the Turks could have caused all kinds of problems for the retiring army. The guns had already been packed up and although the left-hand side of the line was covered by the naval fleet anchored off shore, the right-hand side, the side held by Rackham, was hopelessly exposed. The atmosphere in the trenches was understandably very tense and nerves were shredded, but luckily the Turks did not attack.

As the front-line troops passed through Rackham's lines towards the beaches and the safety of the waiting ships, it became more hopeful that perhaps they might just get away with it. Rackham was one of the last people off the peninsula and he was grateful for calm weather as he bobbed out to sea in a lighter towards his designated destroyer. One of the final acts of the evacuation was to set fire to all of the stores and supplies that were discarded on the beach, and once the ships finally set sail towards Mudros and as the peninsula slowly disappeared over the horizon, Rackham was overcome with a huge sense of sadness at the thought of all the men – colleagues and friends – that he had left behind as casualties, but also a great sense of relief and pride that the evacuation had been executed perfectly.

By 9 January, Rackham had arrived in Mudros Harbour. It was only a short stay and by the end of January they had moved out to Imbros, where they undertook a slight reorganisation. Sub Lieutenant Rackham was now placed within C Company, Hawke Battalion.

A few months later the battalion got the call to move out to France and Rackham disembarked at Marseilles on 18 May 1916. After a short time in a holding camp, Rackham was sent on a training course to become a Lewis gun officer. The first months on the Western Front were pretty easy for Rackham, the Hawke Battalion divided their time between training behind the lines and being posted in various quiet sectors where nothing much happened. It couldn't last forever though, and on 7 October they were given orders to move out of the training camp and march towards the Somme.

By 19 October they had taken up position just in front of the small village of Hamel facing up the Ancre Valley. Across no-man's-land, between 150 and 250 yards away, depending on where you were in the line, were the German front-line trenches. The Hawke Battalion had been chosen to attack the German lines and continue through to a ridge beyond the lines where fortified defensive positions awaited. The quiet and easy days were over.

Zero was set for 5.45 a.m. on 13 November. In the hours running up to the attack the men waited in dark, cramped conditions, squashed into the forward-facing positions ready for the big rush over the top. Rackham was immersed within his own thoughts, wondering if the enemy shells that were still dropping indiscriminately around the trenches were the beginnings of an enemy counter-barrage that would undoubtedly lead to utter carnage in the overcrowded trench systems. Then, at 4 a.m. Rackham squeezed and crept through the massed bodies searching for his platoon, waking them up and making sure they were all ready and knew what they had to do. He was in charge of an ammunition party who were to advance in the immediate wake of the first wave carrying heavy and cumbersome (but vital) ammunition for the fighting men. As his intimate group of men huddled around him, he repeated their orders for the hundredth time, synchronised watches, shook each man's hand and wished them luck. There was nothing more that could be done, other than wait.

One minute to zero … silence. Then a monumental explosion, and the November mist was embellished with the smoke and fumes of war. A split second later and the first wave were scrambling over the precipice and disappearing into the mist. A few minutes later it was Rackham's turn to go over the top.

Almost immediately he was hit in the hand by machine-gun fire. The wound wasn't severe and after a quick trip to a first-aid post to have it looked at he was back in the thick of battle. On his return he cautiously pushed forward, through the smoke, bullets, explosions and the human remains towards the enemy lines. As the mist and smoke slowly cleared it was obvious that the artillery barrage, designed to smash the enemy defence system, had inexplicably failed and dominating what should have been a captured enemy position were significant numbers of enemy machine guns.

The advance had stalled, and unbeknown to the men dying in no-man's-land, they had tried a full frontal assault on one of the most notorious German strongholds on the entire Western Front: the Schwaben Redoubt. The heavy machine guns that defended the redoubt decimated the rows of advancing Hawke Battalion that morning. In the words of the regimental diary, 'The Hawke Battalion after the first few minutes of the attack no longer existed as a unit.' Out of the twenty officers and 415 ratings who had gone into the attack that morning, only nineteen ratings survived. Everyone else was either killed or wounded, including Sub Lieutenant Rackham, although his wound was not too debilitating.

Despite this, small independent pockets of men did manage to get past the redoubt. The decision was eventually made to pull back and renew the attack in the morning with the aid of a few tanks. Tanks were a brand-new weapon at this stage of the war, having debuted only a few months earlier, and the RND had six of them at their disposal in the case of emergencies. This was definitely an emergency.

The following day, reinforced with a handful of tanks, the remnants of the RND charged up the shell-swept hill towards the enemy defence. It was an act of futile defiance, with only two out of the original six tanks operational, but they were met, not with enfilade fire from the strongpoint, but with white flags as the enemy surrendered.

For Rackham, the last twenty-four hours had proved to him three things: first, attacking infantry cannot rely on artillery to smash all of the enemy's defence systems; second, machine guns, along with the barbed wire, dominated the battlefield; and third, the arrival of the armoured vehicle was perhaps the beginning of the answer to combatting the dual issues of wire and machine guns.

After this battle, what was left of the Hawke Battalion (nineteen NCOs and ratings and another 100 or so cooks, transport men and other non-combatants) were sent into the reserve lines for a well-deserved rest and to await reinforcements. On 16 November a memorial service was held for those officers and men of the battalion who had been killed in the recent action. The official battalion diary describes the remnants as a 'very pathetic little battalion'.

Rackham was admitted to 2nd Stationary Hospital, Abbeville, on 24 November to get his wounded hand seen to. He was discharged on 30 November and rejoined his unit the day after. During the ensuing reorganisation Rackham was appointed to the post of assistant adjutant.

The year 1917 dawned with new hope for Rackham, the battalion slowly got back to full strength and by early January they were all ready to go again. The irony wasn't lost on Rackham and his fellow officers when they found themselves marching back towards the Ancre, and by the 23rd they were taking up positions in the line around Beaucourt. The term 'line' here is used in the loosest possible sense as there was no actual line, just a random collection of shell holes, some connected to each other, some isolated. Thankfully, they were there only a matter of days. Their job was to reconnoitre the land and surrounding area in preparation for an attack they would be carrying out in a few weeks' time. By 26 January, Rackham found himself way back behind the lines preparing for the attack.

The objective for this offensive was to attack up the slope behind Beaucourt towards the German trench system, which sat upon a ridge that dominated the local area. The idea being that once this ridge and the ridge beyond were captured the enemy would be forced to retreat. One thing of note about this advance was that zero hour was pencilled in for 11 p.m. on 3 February – it would be a night attack, which was something not often seen on the Western Front.

Rackham's C Company was positioned on the far left of the offensive line and was instructed to join up with the Nelson Battalion to form a defensive flank. However, the Nelsons never received their part of the message and were not in position when the whistles blew to signal the start of the offensive. At around 4 a.m. on 4 February the enemy counterattacked directly into the face of C Company. The left flank was completely 'in the air' and there was a very real danger of a collapse.

C Company were left for the best part of twenty-four hours to repel the enemy on their own. They were freezing, having left their overcoats in the reserve lines, and the casualties were mounting. Rackham and his men were fighting like tigers, but surely it would only be a matter of time before they were overwhelmed. Eventually, reinforcements headed by Commander Shelton arrived on the scene:

> We arrived eventually, and placed the men out along the unpro-tected flank, just in time to stave off another counter-attack. The rum was more than useful, as the men were half starved with the cold, the temperature not far off zero. They had a thundering good tot, which put new life into them.

For his actions that day, Commander Shelton was awarded the DSO. Sub Lieutenant Rackham was also awarded the Military Cross, the citation for which appeared in the *London Gazette* on 26 March 1917:

> For conspicuous gallantry in action. He showed marked ability in preparing gun positions and continually moved from position to position under heavy fire. On occasion he displayed great bravery in going round the whole line during an enemy counter attack.

By the end of 6 February a definite tactical success had taken place. Grandcourt was evacuated and the German retreat had begun.

A fellow RND officer, A.P. Herbert, wrote a poem called the 'The Investiture', which was published in *Punch* in April 1917. Herbert sent an amended copy of the poem (to include Basil's name) to Rackham's mother, explaining that *Punch* wouldn't let him publish it with the name Basil as they didn't like it as much.

After a period of rest, Rackham was back in the thick of it in April 1917. On the evening of 22 April the Hawke Battalion moved up to their assembly positions in preparation for the attack the next day. The objective was the town of Gavrelle. For this show, the battalion was in reserve, in a similar situation to the action in Gallipoli. But this wasn't Gallipoli – this was the Western Front and the rules were different. Whereas the biggest enemy a reserve battalion at Gallipoli was likely to face were the flies, it was a very different situation in France.

On 23 April they were to give the first wave of assaulting troops just a five-minute head start before they were to join in the fight. Rackham, as assistant adjutant, would be slightly behind this reserve wave; he would go across with the HQ party to oversee the consolidation of the (hopefully) captured German lines.

In this situation five minutes wasn't a great deal of time, and when they went over the top laden with ammunition, sandbags, picks, shovels and all manner of other supplies, they quickly found themselves in bitter hand-to-hand fighting along the German parapet with enemy soldiers who, some-how, the initial assaulting wave had failed to clear. Rackham and the rest of the HQ party, including Colonel Whiteman, followed behind at about midday, through an intense enemy artillery bombardment, and entered the enemy trench in a strangely ceremonial manner.

Once in the trench the HQ party were caught in the middle of more shellfire as the German artillery tried to remove the attackers from their trench system. Both Colonel Whiteman and his adjutant became casualties of shrapnel. As a consequence, Rackham was promoted to adjutant and imme-diately helped organise the evacuation of the colonel back towards the nearest dressing station. Tragically, the colonel was wounded again on that tortuous journey, this time fatally, and he would die of his wounds on 3 May.

After this isolated success the Hawkes were pulled back into the reserve and the next few months passed by relatively peacefully. On 30 September, the order was given to get ready to move out. Rackham and the rest of the Hawke Battalion would soon be back out on the road, marching north – towards Passchendaele.

There were only two legitimate routes to carry men and supplies over the part of the front that Rackham now occupied. Practically every waking moment was taken up with preserving the precious wooden duckboard highways. Even when they were intact and working to full capacity, only a fraction of the required men and supplies could get to and from the front – but they were *never* intact. Being in full view of the enemy, these duckboard roads were smashed by enemy artillery day and night.

Reminiscing on his time at Passchendaele, Rackham had one enduring memory:

> … conditions were terrible … physically on the ground … just mud, mud, mud and if you slipped off the mud or a wretched mule slipped off the mud they were virtually sunk. You could get a man out, but you couldn't get a mule out.

During an interview with the Imperial War Museum, the interviewer notes, 'During the interview, he covered his service at Gallipoli and on the Western Front. But when he got to Passchendaele, he broke down in tears. For him, the remembrance of this action was too terrible to contemplate.'

A fellow Hawke officer wrote of the thankless task they all faced at Passchendaele:

> Indiscriminate shelling was carried out to keep the ground liquid for several feet, and prevent the dykes and streams settling into permanent courses, and by bombing and shelling to prevent engineering material from reaching the gun positions.
>
> Our task, then, was a pretty tough one … We strove to construct and maintain an artery upon which the life of a sustained

action could depend … day after day, on arriving on the ground we would find the track which the previous day's work had left firm and ready to receive the planks ploughed up with shells, strewn with broken limbers, dead or foundered mules, dumps of 18-pound shells, and all the litter and debris of the hours of darkness, when the teams proceeding to the batteries had reached the end of the planking and floundered into the mud, sinking deeper and deeper until they had to be abandoned.

Our day's work always started with shooting certain animals abandoned in the mud, and one day as many as twelve had to be dispatched close to the Mont de Hybou before we could proceed with our proper business.

The task, theoretically, was simple. To make a firm track, with ditches on either side at a gradient to carry off the water, and to lay planks upon it, presents no difficulty. But to do this, when each day's work is undone by night, is as unprofitable as Penelope's stitching. Everyday some fresh problem presented itself … And all the time casualties. Casualties on the way up, casualties on the way down, casualties while at work!

Sadly, 1918 wouldn't be much better. Although they moved out of the immediate Passchendaele area, they were rushed to Cambrai to stem the tide after the tank battle there. They found themselves slap-bang in the middle of a German attack, and they were facing a portion of the enemy who just loved to play with their artillery. As 1917 gave way to 1918, the Hawkes were subjected to significant artillery bombardments day after day. Morale was low, the weather was awful and everyday there were more casualties from shellfire. And it was only to get worse …

From the beginning of March, whether they were in support lines, in the old Hindenburg trenches or in the front line, they were shelled from pillar to post and almost continually gassed.

The casualties soon mounted, as indicated from the following excerpts from the war diary of that period:

March 1st, 4.30am: Heavy bombardment on Trescault Ridge.

March 7th: Enemy artillery active thro'out the day on front and support lines. Enemy aircraft active.

March 8th 10am & 11am: Heavy enemy barrage with 5.9s on front and support lines.

March 12th: For 4 hours (from 10pm on 11th to 2am on 12th) the enemy put a very strong concentration of gas in Trescourt and Ribècourt … Casualties 4 officers gassed, 135 ORs gassed.

March 13th: From 11pm on 12th till 2.30am on 13th, concentration of gas shells on Ribècourt. Estimated about 10,000 shells were fired. From 8.15am to 8.45am barrage of gas shells again put down on Ribècourt. D Coy in the catacombs of Ribècourt suffered heavily. Casualties 3 officers gassed, 127 ORs gassed.

March 14th: Night of 13th–14th enemy put down a barrage of gas shells on Unseen Trench & Unseen Support. Casualties 4 officers gassed, 18 ORs gassed.

March 15th: During the night of 14–15th a barrage of gas shells was put down on Unseen Trench and Unseen Support. Casualties 1 officer gassed, 113 ORs gassed.

March 16th: Casualties 16 ORs gassed.

March 17th: Casualties 35 ORs gassed.

And so it went on, until:

> March 20th: Enemy artillery very quiet. An attack was expected by the enemy but our patrols found no signs of enemy movement or activity.

They didn't have to wait long. The very next day the hurricane was let loose. As the Hawke Battalion readied their rifles and gritted their teeth there were only about 380 officers and ratings holding a line that, just a few weeks before, had been held by almost 2,000. They didn't stand a chance.

It quickly became apparent that this was no ordinary offensive. Huge numbers of Germans swarmed over the thinly held trenches, overwhelmed the first line of defence and quickly broke through. The Hawke had no choice but to retreat as best they could – first to Bus, then on to High Wood. They were being chased all the way. In Bus the enemy was observed and a firefight ensued, before they evacuated further to the rear. By the time they had reached High Wood at 7 p.m. on 24 March, enemy patrols were seen no more than 800 yards away from where the remnants of the Hawke Battalion were frantically trying to dig in. It was no use, by the 25th it was obvious they were in grave danger of being outflanked, and when the enemy was seen only 400 yards away from their lines they received the welcome order to retire across open country towards Thiepval.

Rackham, along with a fellow officer, was the last to leave and after making sure the final group of men got on their way they turned their attention to how they were going to get out of that wood. After an eventful scramble across open country, and picking up a couple of other officers along the way, they finally reached safety. When the Hawke Battalion finally took defensive positions in old German trenches south of the

River Ancre during the evening of 25 March there were only five officers and sixty-three ratings present.

On 27 March Rackham was taken sick with gas poisoning. The last week had been particularly trying. In his role as adjutant he had been very active in organising the troops and making sure they were okay through the intense gas bombardments, the enemy attack and subsequent retreat. He had been burned himself several times by the mustard gas, and eventually it took its toll, but not before he had ensured the safe evacuation of all that was left of his battalion. He passed out, and on 29 March he was admitted to 14th General Hospital, Wimereux. From there he was taken back to England where he recovered at the 1st London General Hospital, St Gabriel's College, Camberwell.

At a Medical Board examination in Exeter on 24 May 1918 he was deemed fit again for active service, given three weeks' leave and ordered to report to Aldershot on its expiration. In the meantime, Rackham was awarded a Bar to his Military Cross for his actions during those desperate days of March. The citation for his award appeared in the *London Gazette* on 26 July 1918, and read:

> For conspicuous gallantry and devotion to duty. Although suffering from the effects of gas, he remained at duty and materially assisted in keeping the battalion together. It was only when the enemy's advance had been held up and he was directly ordered to do so, that he went to hospital.

After his three weeks' leave he dutifully reported back. However, he had seen front-line service for the last time in this war; he was taken on to the strength of the 2nd Reserve Battalion and he stayed in Aldershot, where he attended officer training and various gas courses (qualifying as an instructor) before finally rejoining his original battalion for the final advances and ultimate victory. By 6 June the whole of the Royal Naval Division was back on home soil, parading at Horse Guards for the final time in front of the Prince of Wales. Shortly afterwards the division was disbanded, and on 8 June Lieutenant Rackham was demobilised.

Rackham found it tough acclimatising to civilian life and quickly decided that a return to the military would be his best bet. He was delighted to read in the *London Gazette* of 13 December 1920 that he had been appointed to a permanent regular commission as a lieutenant in the Middlesex Regiment.

In 1925 he married Elsie Catchpool, although he continued his military career and by the time the Second World War came knocking he was in command of the 1/7th Middlesex Regiment. His battalion was in the thick of the fighting in Belgium in 1940 and fought continuously in the subsequent withdrawal, being one of the last men to leave Dunkirk. Throughout this trying time his courage, leadership and calmness was an inspiration to his men. By 1941 he had risen to the rank of colonel, second-in-command of the support group to the 9th Armoured Division; he then moved up to brigade commander, based in the UK.

In the run-up to D-Day he was attached to HQ 7th Infantry Brigade as lieutenant colonel (temporary brigadier) and was heavily involved in the administration and preparation for the Allied invasion of Normandy. He was desperately disappointed that he was not allowed to take part in the actual landings themselves on account of his age, but he was, however, awarded the CBE for his role in the preparations:

Was in command of Marshalling Area 'S' at Tilbury throughout the whole of the preparation & mounting of Operation OVERLORD. The task allotted to Brig. Rackham was carried through without a hitch & the whole arrangements worked with great efficiency & smoothness & the success was in very large measure due to the organising ability & excellent work put in by him. The operation was unique in character & demanded initiative & foresight of a high order; Brig. Rackham met all demands made on him with outstanding efficiency & inspired a first-class team.

He formally retired from the army in 1945 and became secretary to the Middlesex Territorial Association. He was also the first president of the Gallipoli Association.

He died in 1988 at his home in Woodbridge, at the age of 91.

13

5441 COMPANY SERGEANT MAJOR FREDERICK WATSON MC, DCM

(2/5TH BATTALION, KING'S OWN YORKSHIRE LIGHT INFANTRY)

Frederick Watson was born in Leeds on 8 November 1878. He enlisted in the King's Own Yorkshire Light Infantry (KOYLI) on 27 February 1897, aged 18, giving his occupation as a mechanic. He signed up for seven years with 'the colours' with a further five years to be served as a reservist. Fred was not a big man, measuring up at 5ft 3½in tall and weighing in at 8½ stones; however, his small stature belied his appetite for adventure and his bravery.

He was awarded a Good Conduct Badge on 27 February 1899 (the second anniversary of his enlistment) and little more than two months later, on 6 May, he was promoted to lance corporal. On the fourth anniversary of his enlistment, in 1901, he was awarded a second Good Conduct Badge and was promoted to corporal on 4 April of that year. In December 1901 he was posted from the 1st to the 2nd Battalion of the KOYLI and sent to South Africa, where the British were fighting the Boer farmers.

It was in South Africa that he first got himself into trouble when, on 4 May 1902, he was given a severe reprimand for 'Neglect of Duty whilst in charge of a Block House'. Despite this, three months later, on 14 August, he was promoted to sergeant. He continued to serve in South Africa for a further four months, until October 1902 when he was posted with the rest of the battalion to Malta. While in Malta his terms of service were amended so that he was to serve the full twelve years 'with the colours'.

In March 1904 the battalion was transferred to Crete, where it stayed for a further year before coming back home in March 1905. On 21 July 1906 Fred found himself in trouble again, being given a further severe reprimand when caught 'Gambling in camp [at Bisley] about 9.45pm'.

Despite these misdemeanours, on 18 January 1908, a month short of the eleventh anniversary of his enlistment and with still over a year of his engagement to run, he signed on to serve for another ten years. A major factor here was the promise of adventure in West Africa, as he was soon seconded to the Northern Nigeria Regiment. He served in West Africa for a year, returning home in April 1909, and later that year, on 9 June, he married Ada Ellen Taylor in Ravensthorpe Parish church.

Returning to the 2nd Battalion he spent part of the next period of his service in Ireland. It was while in Cork that he was to receive a 'Reprimand [for] neglect of duty when in charge of a fatigue party (allowing men to fall out)'. It seems that, rather than keeping the men working, he allowed them to rest but was found out by his sergeant major.

On 24 May 1912 he was posted to the 5th (Territorial) Battalion, which recruited one of its companies in Goole, where he would work as a sergeant drill instructor during the first months of the First World War. It was in this town that his three sons, George, Morris and Jack, were born.

When war broke out in 1914 he was a likely candidate to go to France as part of the initial BEF with the 2nd KOYLI. However, experienced soldiers like Watson were desperately required to train the new recruits who were flooding into the army, and as a result he was promoted to company sergeant major (CSM) and kept back as a drill instructor. Rather than being posted to one of the Kitchener battalions, he remained in England with the 1/5th Battalion. He was disappointed but set his sights on moving out to France in the spring of 1915, which is when the 1/5th was earmarked to move out to the Western Front. However, when the time came it was again decided that he was more useful being kept back to help train the second-line battalions that were being formed. As a result he was moved to the 62nd (2nd West Riding) Division, which was being formed as a back-up to the initial 49th Division.

The 62nd Division was kept back for coastal defence duties until the end of 1916 when orders were received to proceed overseas, which it duly did in January 1917. Company Sergeant Major Watson would finally get over to the Western Front with the 2/5th KOYLI. In early February the division was told to make itself ready for taking over trenches in the Beaumont-Hamel area of the Somme. The history of the 62nd Division describes the conditions:

> Trenches as such did not exist, for they had been obliterated by the concentrated fire of the guns … The front line was held by a series of posts which resembled islands in a sea of mud. Shell holes pock-marked the ground, often overlapping one another and where pathways existed between them they were but a few inches wide. The holes were full of water and more than one man lost his life through slipping off the pathway into the slimy mass which engulfed him.

In order to save men and materials, the German High Command decided a new trench system would be required and in September 1916 a site for this was selected about 25 miles behind their front line. This new line, known to the British as the Hindenburg Line, saved the Germans about 25 miles of front line which would not therefore have to be manned. On 4 February 1917 the order was given by the German High Command to prepare for the withdrawal.

The Allies were surprised by the withdrawal and gave orders for the Germans to be harried during their retirement. The Germans were determined to give up the ground at their own pace and left behind stubborn rear guards who caused casualties to the troops following, among whom happened to be men from the 62nd Division. It was at this time that Fred Watson earned the first of his gallantry medals.

On 6 March, the battalion moved up into support at Bois d'Holland (on the eastern edge of Beaucourt) and the next day moved up to the front line, which was at that time between the villages of Miramont and Achiet-le-Petit. On the right of the battalion was the 10th Essex Regiment, part of 18th (Eastern) Division. The war diary of the 2/5th KOYLI for 8 March describes how Second Lieutenant Atkin led a daylight patrol, an action for which he earned the DCM. The diary goes on, 'CSM [Company Sergeant Major] F.W. Watson established a post in Resurrection Trench to assist the 10th Essex to carry out a bombing attack. A previous attempt had failed. CSM Watson awarded the D.C.M.' Fred Watson's citation for the DCM appeared in the *London Gazette* on 17 April 1917:

> For conspicuous gallantry and devotion to duty. He succeeded in establishing a post at a critical time under the most trying conditions. He has at all times set a splendid example of courage and determination.

Shortly after he was awarded his DCM the existing 2/5th KOYLI regimental sergeant major (RSM) was given a commission, and a replacement RSM was therefore required. Fred was chosen, and on 2 May 1917 Fred was promoted to temporary RSM for the duration of the war. The promotion was made the day before the Second Battle of Bullecourt, in which the battalion was engaged. Bullecourt (part of the Battle of Arras) was to be the 62nd Division's first major fight. Unfortunately things went very badly, so much so that Fred's commanding officer in the 2/5th KOYLI, Lieutenant Colonel W. Watson, was killed, his place being taken by the second-in-command, Major O.C. Watson.

Fred was not destined to keep his exalted rank for long. As well as enjoying the odd perk and a good deal of power over the rank and file, there was a lot of pressure on the senior NCO in the battalion. Perhaps he was unable to cope with the demands made upon him, or possibly he was just unlucky to be caught, but on 4 August 1917 Fred was discovered drunk while on duty. He was placed under arrest and tried by a field general court martial a week later. Not surprisingly, Fred was found guilty as charged. The sentence bestowed upon him was to be reduced to the rank of sergeant, a sentence which was quite lenient, based on the grounds of his previous long and distinguished service.

From the end of September to the middle of November, Fred left the battalion and acted as an instructor for the division in the reserve lines. Upon rejoining the 2/5th KOYLI he was once again appointed to the acting rank of CSM. Fred was allowed home on leave between 22 December 1917 and 5 January 1918. On returning to his battalion he was confirmed in his rank of CSM. Around this time there was a major reorganisation within the British Army, and one of the results of this was that the 1/5th KOYLI was merged with

Fred's 2/5th KOYLI. The merged battalion was renamed the 5th KOYLI and remained within the 62nd Division.

After a sustained period of time in reserve or in quiet sectors, Watson and the rest of the 5th Battalion were to be given the chance to take part in some serious action. They had been chosen to attack the much vaunted Hindenburg Line. The attack was pencilled in for 3.45 a.m. on 3 May and immediately after the nod was given the officers and staff got busy. By 1.45 a.m. on 3 May everything was set – Fred had taken up his position in the attack formation between the railway cutting and the front line of posts. He was among hundreds of men huddled in no-man's-land with practically no cover or defence. There was nothing to do but be as quiet as possible and try and snatch a bit of sleep while waiting for zero and hope that the Germans didn't get twitchy and start lobbing over shells, as they were very, very exposed.

Luckily no such thing happened and at zero it was the British guns that barked into life, smashing the enemy lines to pieces. The night was pitch dark and a strong wind blew the smoke and dust of the barrage back into the faces of Fred and the other attackers. It became almost impossible to keep direction and there was consequent confusion as they progressed along no-man's-land. When they got to the wire they found that, on the whole, it was still in one piece and as a result the massed ranks of attacking troops were forced to move laterally along the battlefield trying to find gaps in the wire so they could get through.

Confusion reigned and in an effort to try and sort it out, Lieutenant Colonel O.C. Watson, already badly wounded, went out to the wire to rally his men and try to reorganise them back into an effective fighting force. With the help of fellow officers he restored a semblance of order and reorganised the advance. It was an act of extraordinary courage and leadership that ultimately saw him recommended (and accepted) for the Victoria Cross. He would never get the chance to receive his award though. He he was killed at about 4.20 a.m. Losing a leader such as Lieutenant Colonel Watson was disastrous for the attack, which quickly became disorganised once more and failed to make any headway in the face of fierce machine-gun and shell fire. They were getting cut to pieces on the German wire. The attack failed miserably with the 5th suffering 271 casualties that morning.

By now, Fred had amassed a total of twenty-one years' service in the army and he would, under normal conditions, have been discharged. But this wasn't a normal situation and Fred was a vastly experienced NCO of huge value to an army made up of large numbers of amateurs. Even had he wanted to, it is unlikely he would have been able to avoid further military service and he therefore signed on again 'for the duration of the war'. After a month's leave at home, when he saw his wife and three sons for what was to be the last time, he returned to his battalion on 11 June and recommenced his duties as CSM for D Company.

In July 1918, the 62nd Division was transferred to the south to assist the French in beating off the massive German attacks that were being made in a final all-out attempt to win the war. The division arrived in the sector of the River Marne on 17 July and was soon taking part in one of the French counter-attacks. It is against this background that Fred's service record gives further details of his last period with the army.

On 20 July 1918 the 5th Battalion was earmarked to attack the area around Bois-de-Reims and Château-de-Commetréuil. It was during this attack that Fred won his Military Cross. The official citation for the award appeared in the *London Gazette* of 7 November 1918:

5441 CSM Frederick William Watson, D.C.M., Yorkshire Light Infantry: For conspicuous gallantry and good leadership. When the officers of two platoons became casualties he took command and led the men forward with great dash and skill. He was cut off with part of his platoon but fought his way back to his company. His courage and resolution were remarkable and his cheerfulness inspired all who were with him.

The last of the German assaults was beaten back and it was now the turn of the Allies to counter-attack. This commenced on 8 August 1918 and was to be the start of the so-called 'hundred days', when the Allies forced the Germans all the way back to the borders of Germany itself. This series of victories was not, however, without its price and it was during this period that Fred Watson was to lose his life.

Orders for an attack by the 62nd Division at the village of Mory (near Achiet-le-Grand) were received during the afternoon of 25 August. This was to commence at 6 a.m. on 26 August following a barrage by British artillery. Further orders were received on the afternoon of 26 August for a continuation of the attack the next day at 7.30 a.m. The battalion's objectives were a sunken road running north–south about half a mile west of the village of Vraucourt. On the sunken road, at a crossroads, lay a sugar factory.

Fred Watson's D Company was to lead the attack with B Company in support. The assembly positions were to be on the railway east of Mory and, to avoid the planned British artillery barrage, the attacking companies were ordered to stay to the north of the sunken road leading east from Mory.

Everything was going well until the attacking troops came to the road junction north-east of the factory. They were hit by fire from German machine-gunners who had managed to survive the artillery barrage. The war diary of the 5th KOYLI states:

During the attack 2/Lt. Logan with his Company Sergeant Major and one runner showed great coolness in capturing seven officers and one hundred other ranks – practically the whole of Battalion HQ – in dugouts.

The war diary continues:

On ascertaining the situation Lieut. R. A. Houghton who was in command of the support company, collecting what men he could from his own company and details of other units, took up a defensive line which he was ordered to hold at all costs. Parties of the attacking company ('D') who were absolutely cut off dribbled in during the afternoon and at night along Banks Trench and around the left flank.

During the attack, the 5th KOYLI suffered twenty-four other ranks killed, plus four officers and 114 other ranks wounded. One of the fatal casualties was CSM Fred Watson.

Fred's wife, Ada, received a letter at their house which told how Fred '… met his death from an enemy machine gun bullet, which hit him in the back of the neck. He died in a few minutes.' Fred was aged 39 when he was killed and is buried in Gomiecourt South Cemetery.

14

LIEUTENANT COLONEL GRAHAM SETON HUTCHISON DSO, MC

(MACHINE GUN CORPS)

Graham Seton Hutchison was born, along with his twin brother, Legh Richmond, and an elder brother by one year, Colin Alexander Gordon, in a house known as Three Gables in Fitzjohn's Avenue, Hampstead, in 1890. He had a large extended family with significant civic and military traditions: his father, James Alexander, held a leading position in one of the principal merchant banks in London and indeed the family had been closely linked in one way or another to the City of London for hundreds of years, supplying the city with four generations of common councillors, three generations of aldermen, three sheriffs and two lord mayors.

As well as being a successful businessman in the City, his father was also a noted alpine climber and was one of the first people to climb the Matterhorn. However, his alpine adventures took a severe toll on his health and after a long illness he passed away aged 53 – Graham was just 6 years old. The advantage of having a large family meant that uncles, aunts and grandparents were able to help bring up the three Hutchison boys, ably assisted by the obligatory nanny and butler.

Early school wasn't much fun for the young Hutchison. While their older brother went off to boarding school at St Clare's in Walmer, the twins boarded at Heddon Court. The twins had contrasting experiences in their first few years at school. While Legh prospered, Graham hated it and in a letter home to his mother he couldn't have put any more plainly how he felt: 'I hate all the boys ... it is a great disappointment to me to have to stay at school with all these nasty boys.' He was an introverted and awkward child, often picked on, and as such did not prosper. After a few years he was moved to join his elder brother at St Clare's. The change in scenery seems to have done the young Hutchison good. He matured quickly, both physically and mentally, and by the age of 10 was a key member of the first teams in football, cricket and hockey.

He returned to Heddon Court at the age of 12, but instead of reverting back to the awkward, shy boy he had been when he was there originally, he grew from strength to strength. He became a prefect and continued to show athletic prowess, breaking many track and field records during his tenure. When he moved to Bradfield College it was his sporting prowess and the admiration that the top athletes enjoyed at the school that made him choose the Army House. This house was full of the best sporting talent in the school, as well as aspiring military leaders in waiting. He would now be educated towards a military career.

Although not a top-grade scholar across the board, he proved himself a capable enough student, especially in history and geography. However, he was suspended from the school for playing the banjo outside the house master's study during the night. He was sent home to his mother in disgrace, the house master refusing to keep him in the college a day longer. In order for him to pass his exams for Sandhurst he instead had to undergo costly private tutelage.

He passed through Sandhurst and in the last week of 1910 sailed for Egypt on the Troopship *Rohilla* to join up with the 1st Battalion King's Own Scottish Borderers. Weeks and weeks of drill, parade and rifle exercises filled the days until, being a noted draughtsman, he was entrusted with conducting a survey of the banks of the Nile between Khartoum and Shendi. This month-long trek through the desert with camels, camping among the patchwork of tiny villages, bathing in the Nile, and the long marches in the searing heat was to be one of his most memorable times and would stay with him throughout his life.

In February 1911, the battalion was earmarked for a switch to service in India and thus entrained for Port Sudan, where it boarded a troopship bound for Bombay. During his time in Bombay he became slightly disillusioned with life in the army, a feeling not helped when he had an altercation with a fellow officer who stabbed him several times with his sword. Hutchison began to muse over some plans and ideas to free himself from what he saw as the monotony of army life. However, he was duly promoted – on the back of an essay on military strategy – and appointed staff officer to the Durbar Committee.

The Delhi Durbar was to be held in December 1911 to officially crown the newly enthroned George V and his wife Queen Mary as Emperor and Empress of India. The king and queen planned to attend the durbar in person wearing their coronation robes, an unprecedented event in both Indian and imperial history and held with unparalleled pomp and glamour. Practically every ruling prince, nobleman and person of note was invited to attend the ceremonies to pay obeisance to their sovereign in person, and it was down to Hutchison and a few other staff officers to ensure the durbar was organised properly and ran smoothly.

It was just the kind of high-profile project he could get stuck into and he threw himself wholeheartedly into it. It was a complete success. However, it was nothing more than a reprieve and once it was over only served to reinforce his growing conviction that he could, and should, do a bit more with this life. Without a war (which seemed very unlikely at that point in time), the uneventful career of a regimental soldier held few attractions for Hutchison, and so he decided to throw in the towel on his army career and seek adventure and fortune in Australia.

He sailed into Sydney Harbour as a young man with the world at his feet. However, his dreams were quickly shattered as he found it very difficult to put his considerable skills to work in his newly adopted homeland. He managed to get a string of low-paid temporary jobs, but none of them were able to keep him in the lifestyle he thought appropriate for an officer of the British Army, and as work of any description dried up he soon found himself at the bottom of both the social and economic ladders. He made several attempts to withdraw his resignation and regain his commission in the army, but these attempts failed.

With the Brisbane strike he saw an opportunity to escape and hotfooted it over to Brisbane to work as a strike breaker. The work was hard and he was often beaten by the strikers, but he managed to earn enough to get him on a boat out of there and back to England.

By July 1912 he was back in England. Once again he tried to regain his commission and, once again, he failed. He kept plugging away though, reaching out to all his contacts and former army colleagues to see if anyone could pull strings on his behalf. Eventually his persistence paid off and the call came.

On 19 April 1913 Hutchison was gazetted as a lieutenant in the 3rd Battalion Argyll and Sutherland Highlanders.

Shortly after joining up he attended a musketry school which introduced him to the machine gun, of which he was greatly impressed, specifically the rate and accuracy of fire. However, it wasn't long before he had the urge to seek more adventure in another distant part of the empire and he soon found himself accepted in the British South Africa Police and in October 1913 was on board a Union-Castle liner.

While serving in Rhodesia it quickly became apparent to Hutchison that there was no intelligence department at the military HQ and there was little or no co-operation or communication between the military outposts and territories bordering Rhodesia. This, to Hutchison's eyes, was a major oversight which was putting the territory at risk of native risings and invasion. He wrote up his findings, presented a full report to the commanding officer and soon found himself appointed intelligence officer.

His work as intelligence officer was to take on huge significance as the months rolled on and war beckoned on the horizon. Germany had a significant military presence in South-West Africa and was making everyone nervous. Over the months, though, Hutchison worked hard to put together detailed intelligence reports of both the surrounding geography and enemy organisation and disposition.

As Britain declared war on 4 August 1914, Hutchison was immediately offered a commission with the 1st Rhodesia Regiment but he was ordered to report to London. Once he arrived he tried to get on the next draft out to France, having heard that the BEF had taken a bit of a mauling at Mons and Le Cateau. However, to his dismay he was ordered to Gravesend to take charge of musketry training. He trained reservists of all shapes and sizes – old men and young boys, the majority of whom had never held a gun or rifle in their lives. Hutchison enjoyed the role of whipping these men into some sort of shape but, when the call came to move out to France, he didn't need to be asked twice.

Those first few months were hard. Although they had missed the bloodbaths of Mons and Le Cateau and casualties were not especially high, the discomfort suffered by the troops was intense in the first months. The weather was terrible and the army was not structured for trench warfare. The soldiers didn't have the supplies and equipment they needed to survive and live in the trenches.

Hutchison kept a private diary of his time in the trenches and paints a vivid picture of the reality of warfare in the early months of the war:

November 22nd. Battalion went into trenches. remained in reserve in Bois Grenier. Billeted in house with sheets. Chucked away sheets, too cold, no windows. Bats flew into the light. Much shelling by day and heavy sniping. Farm and haystacks behind our trenches set on fire by shells, where our rations were stored.

November 25th. Very dark night. Sentries jumpy. Dog watch again. Digging all day. Our Battery behind Houplines at 11.30am fired on farm-houses opposite D Company. Effective fire … Germans retaliated by firing salvos of Jack Johnsons … At dusk went with three men to investigate farm in front of lines evacuated by Germans, brought back potatoes, entrenching tools and a kitchen … Germans threw searchlights across our lines. No mail. Hideously dirty and unshaven. Dog watch again. Raining hard.

November 26th. Hard day entrenching. Rain continues. Rifles in fearful state. Bolts impossible to open, ammunition too dirty to place in rifles. Threw out a sap 30 yards to left front to be operated by night if foggy so as to keep pulse of company steady. Only three hours' rest.

December 4th. Heavy shelling and heavy rain. Collapsing dugouts and falling traverses. Trenches deep in water and slime.

There was a brief respite on Christmas Day when both sides took part in an impromptu armistice:

December 25th. Heavy frost and thick mist. Every man received a Christmas card from H.M. the King and H.M. the Queen, bearing the message 'With our best wishes for Christmas 1914. May God protect you and bring you safe home. Mary R. George R.I.' A great rum issue. Many expressions of goodwill. In the afternoon the war ceased and we advanced across our trenches and chatted with the Germans. Most amusing. Can this be war? Some had played football against Glasgow Celtic. All were certain of victory in about six months, for Germany and the end of the war. They gave us cigars and cap badges … Mother sent me a hot-water bottle. Everyone very jealous.

But it was only a brief break, and January 1915 saw a return to the monotony and hardship of trench warfare – even for the officers. But, it is clear that there was a great spirit and a great bond of togetherness within this group of 'Old Contemptibles' and this spirit helped the small force hold off the massed ranks of the German Army:

January 13th. Bitterly cold night. Freezing hard. Working party 9pm–1am. High cutting wind made it almost too cold to work. R.E. sent no material worth having. Awful night. Very wet and freezing. Rubbed each others feet with oil. Could not lie down. Huddled ourselves in a blanket and prayed for morning. Most of B Company sick and getting frost bitten.

January 14th. Vigorous sniping. Four men badly hit on working party. Wickedly cold. Tried to sleep on a board laid over a minenwerfer hole. Kept each other warm and hugged the water bottle – miraculously filled. A bit feverish.

It wasn't long before Hutchison was recalled back to Britain – Edinburgh to be precise – to help train up new recruits. His intimate knowledge of the machine gun was rare and valuable and he was appointed as officer in charge of both musketry and machine-gun instruction. While he was instructing he secured a transfer, in June 1915, as brigade machine-gun officer to the 100th Infantry Brigade of the 33rd Division.

The division went to France in September and moved into the front line beside La Bassée Canal in October. In this part of the line rumours of spies were rife and in one instance, when Hutchison returned back to the lines at dawn, he was arrested on suspicion of being a spy by a group of nervous riflemen and very nearly shot. To avoid a repeat of such scenarios, Hutchison was awarded with a pass, signed by the staff captain, which read, 'To all concerned. This officer is not a spy but the BMGO 100th Inf. Bde. AAA. He possesses an identity disc to this effect and is tattooed on the left forearm AAA. His name is Captain Hutchison. A and S.H. AAA.' The message worked and Hutchison was not shot or arrested on account of being a spy again.

In January 1916 the War Office sanctioned the formation of the Machine Gun Corps and Hutchison was ordered back to Grantham to take over command of the 100th Machine Gun Company. He was back in the line in January 1916 with his new machine-gun section, occupying the sector near Cuinchy. During this time the activities of the new section were limited to raids and a lot of practice with the new unit as part of the bigger brigade. In early July, however, they were moved down the line to the Somme.

By the night of 13 July Hutchison and the rest of the section were resting near Fricourt on the edge of the old German front-line system. The next day they marched, with Hutchison at the head of the column, through the tortured landscapes of the first stages of the Somme battle, past burned-out ambulances, abandoned stretchers and the rotting and bloated bodies of dead soldiers as well as smashed buildings and trees. By noon, the company had reached their lines and immediately set about getting accustomed to their new surroundings. Across the valley could be seen the leafy edge of High Wood, and further to the left was the village of Martinpuich.

Hutchison was ordered to Brigade HQ where he was given orders. The whole battalion would attack at 9.30 a.m. the next morning. The objectives were High Wood, Martinpuich and then on towards Bapaume. This, finally, was the piece of action Hutchison had joined up for all those years ago.

Ground reconnaissance on the eve of the attack brought bad news – very bad news. The Germans had laid several belts of barbed wire in front of their lines and it was largely untouched. Hidden in long grass it was a considerable obstacle. Hutchison and his fellow officers were angry. They knew the likely result of a full-frontal infantry attack against uncut wire, over ground that would likely be enfiladed by machine guns and hammered by enemy artillery. It would be nothing short of carnage.

In the morning, as the infantry went forward at 9.30, their fears of the previous evening came to sharp fruition. From Hutchison's vantage point on the front he saw at first hand the effect of that uncut wire on the attacking infantry:

I, looking across the valley to my left flank, could see the men of the 1st Queen's passing up the slope to Martinpuich. Suddenly they wavered and a few of the foremost attempted to cross some obstacles in the grass. They were awkwardly lifting their legs over a low wire entanglement. Some two hundred men, Major

Palmer at their head, had been brought to a standstill at this point. A scythe seemed to cut their feet from under them, and the line crumpled and fell, stricken by machine-gun fire. Those in support wavered, then turned to fly. There was no shred of cover and they fell in their tracks as rabbits fall at a shooting battue.

It was Hutchison's role to closely support the attacking infantry and give covering fire. He led his men over the top, hot in the footsteps of the first waves:

As we rose to our feet a hail of machine-gun bullets picked here an individual man, there two or three, and swept past us … On my right Huxley, commanding a section, had perished and all his men, with the exception of one who came running towards me, the whole of the front of his face shot away. On my left two other sections had been killed almost to a man, and I see the tripods of the guns with legs waving in the air, and ammunition boxes scattered among the dead.

By 10 a.m. it was obvious that the general attack had failed and only a few of Hutchison's company remained; and then, as if it could not get any worse for the stricken soldiers lying wounded in no-man's-land, the Germans brought up a number of field guns and started to fire shells, practically at point-blank range, directly into the massed ranks of the wounded British attackers. They didn't stand a chance.

Quickly Hutchison got his machine gun up and working and trained it on the gun battery, cutting down the men who were working the guns. Despite neutralising the guns, the British attack had stalled under intense small arms and machine-gun fire. Realising the futility of continuing any further attempt at taking the wood, Hutchison set about rounding up as many men as possible and brought them back to a small chalk quarry that offered a semblance of cover. The motley crew of survivors ducked down in the quarry as the battle raged all about them until, around 5 p.m., the guns seemed to stop. The hysteria and mayhem of explosions had been replaced with an eerie calm, except for the pitiful whimpering of wounded soldiers crying for help in various parts of no-man's-land.

Hutchison looked about him at the shattered men he had collected and organised them in preparation for a renewed attack while the guns were quiet. Slowly, in short rushes, taking extra equipment and rations from the dead as they passed them, they wriggled closer and closer to the outer edge of High Wood. Not a shot was being aimed their way, although the machine-gun, rifle and artillery fire still crashed down on either flank. As they neared the edge of the wood, they fixed bayonets and ruthlessly cleared the enemy trench, disposing of the handful of German soldiers that were still in occupation.

Now the trench was in British hands. Quickly the small group reversed the trench and set up defensive positions utilising an enemy machine gun. A runner was sent back to the lines to request reinforcements while they waited for the expected retaliation. They held on, and help reached them several hours later. When Hutchison finally got back to the dugout he had left early that morning, he was told to report to Brigadier General Baird.

'Sit down Hutchison,' invited the general and poured him a large whisky. 'Drink that.' After a pause the general continued, 'You've done very well ... very well. I did not think it possible to reach High Wood. How many men were with you?'

'Forty-one sir,' replied Hutchison. 'They are all back now.'

For this action Captain Hutchison was awarded the Military Cross, the citation for which appeared in the *London Gazette* on 25 August 1916:

For conspicuous gallantry in action at the German Switch, France on the 17th–18th July, 1916. It was largely due to his fine example that his machine-gun company rendered conspicuous service under most trying conditions.'

There followed a well-earned period of rest behind the lines, before being posted to Arras and pushed into the attack on the Hindenburg Line, where he was involved in bitter hand-to-hand fighting, losing a lot of men.

In June 1917 he was withdrawn from the line once more and was promoted to divisional machine-gun officer, just before being pushed into the line at Passchendaele, where he spent the entire winter of 1917–18 and took part in the Battle of the Menin Road Ridge:

The maps with which I was presented prior to battle betrayed nothing of the chaos, which at every yard of the reconnaissance or attack mocked the eye … Gone were the chateaux, farms and woods of which it spoke … With the aid of a compass I learned the general direction of the attack objective. We would go east from astride the Menin Road by Herenthage Chateau, I noted a derelict tank – thank heavens for that landmark – and an unburied corpse or two which marked the track from Holyborne. Then I returned to my horses. The map sheet was a fair deceiver. But a bogged tank, unburied dead, and a spray of vomiting mud along the horizon gave me the lie of the land …

I found myself in command of the four Divisional Machine-Gun Companies, grouped with others in support of the 23rd Division, whose infantry attack upon Inverness Copse and Polygon Wood, with the added objectives of Passchendaele and Westroosebeke, was to precede the passage of the 33rd Division into the open country beyond.

I had made my first reconnaissance on the morning of the 18th September. From the following day until the 27th, we were occupied in transporting hundreds of thousands of rounds of ammunition to the barrage positions. Over the very slushy ground it required two men to carry each ammunition box. The Divisional Ammunition Column sent up no less than 700,000 rounds on pack mules as far as Holybone, a considerable feat of organisation and patience. From this spot, under sudden and violent shell-storms, or subject to the annoyance of being sniped by field guns, my machine-gunners manhandled the boxes across a mile of shell-pocked land to the positions. The burden was most severe, following, as it did, a march from bivouacs over the broken, pitted, mud-covered track of eight miles …

The position of my machine-gun batteries lay in the middle of the German barrage line, and I suffered very heavy casualties, losing during the morning the officers commanding each one of my Companies, and many valuable N.C.O.s and men. Having completed its role … now depleted in men, and without tried commanders, we were to play a more important part as Infantry accompanying the assault. The men were exhausted.

Whatever losses I had incurred, the orders to advance were clear and concise. The barrage position of the guns was to be moved forward, so soon as the Tower Hamlets Ridge had been gained, to the edge of Inverness Copse. This movement implied not only carrying the guns forward a further mile over territory ankle, sometime knee deep in slush, but bringing up also a further half million rounds of ammunition to serve the guns in the coming fight. The task was probably the most arduous which those under my command were ever asked to perform. Under heavy fire, in which fresh casualties were sustained, by nightfall guns and ammunition had been placed in their new positions, and sighted to fulfil the new barrage charts.

In preparation for the secondary advance, Hutchison found himself in a captured German pillbox which was being used as the headquarters for the 2nd Worcestershires. While he was there the pillbox suffered a direct hit and Hutchison's batman received a really nasty wound:

I carried a bottle of spirit to my junior. He was conscious; a big man, heavily built, and of great strength. I raised and supported him to the 'pill-box'. The candlelight showed a gaping wound gushing blood. The shoulder-blade was pulp, and field glasses and case were embedded in the mess. We dared not remove them, but plugged the hole with fat shell dressings, great wads of antiseptic gauze.

'I'll go down the line now, Sir' said my subordinate. 'I'm a nuisance here.' He rose to his feet and staggered out into the black hurricane.

How often were men torn between duty and friendship. [It was] against the rules to take a wounded man down the line. He must wait for stretcher bearers, or chance the aid of a man slightly hurt to help him on his way. This wound was hideous … If I left him he would bleed to death, and I love his courageous, ever-cheerful self. I, of all men, could not take him. My duty was already overcharged. My lads had scattered to their rendezvous. I could not leave him.

I slipped an arm round him and place his around my shoulders. We floundered back, skirting the edge of Inverness Copse, on the rear side of which lay my barrage batteries. I talked incessantly, any rubbish, to cheer him and to give myself good heart, as the shells plunged and the hot metal hissed and whizzed by. He did not reply, just plugged on, breath coming in heavy gasps. The pace grew slower, his weight bowed upon me … 'Sorry' he gasped, as he lurched and we nearly fell to our knees in the muck. I felt him strengthen – sheer indomitable will. I hulloaed to my batteries. My voice was lost in the shrieking maelstrom. Its fury had even increased, for the hour of dawn approached … I came to a battery position suddenly. Quick hands took my burden, as the unquenchable spirit slipped into unconsciousness … I sent two men from my perilously depleted force to carry my companion to the Aid Post. I could serve a gun myself …

At 3.30am just before dawn the extraordinary happened. With outstanding gallantry the German attacked just as we ourselves were preparing to leap to the assault … I witnessed an astonishing sight. Dense masses of German troops were pouring down the hillside against our Brigades waiting to assault. Suddenly the independent machine-gun company's batteries opened fire. The range was almost point blank … So heavily did this (German) company suffer that its commander, who withdrew his company in perfect order to a new position was assisted only by his one surviving officer, who was badly wounded, and one NCO …

The SOS signal was seen at every point along our lines. Our guns of all calibres and machine-guns immediately opened fire. Following this bombardment, the enemy attacked in mass formation upon our lines, no less than six Divisions being used in this attack on our Divisional front. On the right the posts of the 1st Queen's were over-whelmed, the enemy debouching from the village of Gheluvelt armed with flame-throwers … The men of the 1st Middlesex and the 93rd Highlanders on the left flank met the Bavarian wave with Lewis guns, bombs, and at the point of the bayonet. The resistance was insufficient and the attack swept on …

It was during a lull in the attack that a dishevelled signaller from Headquarters, penetrating the barrage, arrived at my Headquarters. I tore open the sealed envelope to discover not the information which I sought as to the position of the advance, but an order that I should forthwith report the number of tins of plum jam consumed by the units under my command since my last report.

Late in the afternoon it was determined to renew the assault, for by now it was plain that the German counter-attack had been only partly successful ... Fresh troops from the Brigade in reserve, two battalions of Scottish Rifles and one of Royal Fusiliers came up platoon by platoon in shell formation, even so sustaining heavy losses during the earliest stages of the advance ... Beyond Polygon Wood the Australians ... threw themselves to the assault. the stormed across pitted ground and as they advanced taking numbers of prisoners they reached the companies of Middlesex and Argylls, who, sustaining their positions had fought off eleven German attacks ...

So successful was the renewed drive ... that the supports were able to carry forward to the original Divisional objective. Not only had we withstood the fierce attacks of superior forces, but, overwhelming them, had carried all the objectives planned for our own assault.

I brought out of action but one-third of the men who had first rested beside the lake at Dickebusch.

After some well-earned time in reserve, Hutchison and his machine guns got the call to move south on 29 March 1918. The enemy had launched an offensive of epic proportions and it was all hands to the pump. He was in the line by the morning of 12 April.

During the morning of the 12th, Hutchison took part in a cycle reconnaissance of this immediate area. It wasn't long before his reconnaissance party rode directly into the teeth of an enemy advance. He commandeered a field ambulance and sped back to headquarters to organise the movement of his guns up to the front to help with the resistance:

In Meteren there was an A.S.C. [Army Service Corps] motor lorry column. I requested the use of a lorry, but the officer refused it. I hit him on the head with the butt of my revolver, and instructed the driver, Sharples, a splendid young fellow who rendered yeoman assistance to the Division during the next few days, to drive off.

We halted at my farm-house and within a few minutes half a company of machine-gunners, guns and ammunition ... had been packed into the lorry ... We drove straight on over the ridge on which stood the Hoegenmacker Mill, which became the fulcrum of the fighting, where we surprised in the ditch the advance guard of the enemy. From our seat beside the driver, Harrison and I loosened off our revolvers and killed the gun crew, all German storm troops and captured their machine gun.

While hurrying to take up his position, his onrushing lorry of guns and gunners came across masses of British Infantry soldiers retiring in complete disorder. What happened next were the couple of instances that probably earned him the nickname 'the mad major':

At the revolver point I halted one battalion of North Country troops, commanded by a young major, and ordered them to turn about and occupy the Hoegenmacker Ridge. Three times I gave my order and put it also in writing. Each time I was refused. Finally I gave the officer, whose men refused to accept any order except through one of their own officers, two minutes in which to decide, with the alternative of being shot out of hand. At the end of the those two minutes I struck him; and the Regimental Sergeant Major said to me, 'That is what we have been waiting for all day, sir.' He led the company up to the Ridge, though they proved but a feeble defence and leaked away in driblets during the night.

Immediately afterwards, Hutchison pushed his own machine-gun company into the breech in an effort to stem the tide.

After an hour's intense action, he made another reconnaissance and discovered an estaminet full of British Infantry stragglers, all drunk. 'We routed them out, and with a machine gun trained on them sent them forward towards the enemy. They perished to a man.'

By the evening of 12 April, despite huge pressure from the enemy the wafer-thin line in the sector was continuous and had held – just. Dawn on 13 April was shrouded in mist. Using this as cover, the Germans launched a massive attack in the centre of Hutchison's sector. The line buckled and Hutchison was in danger of being surrounded. He was running out of ammunition and losing men up and down the line, with no reinforcements coming his way. By early afternoon the situation was looking desperate until, out of nowhere, limbers of ammunition and supplies were galloped through a hail of enemy shell and machine-gun fire to feed the various gun positions, literally saving the day.

On 14 April it was a case of déjà vu with another heavy dawn raid by the enemy. This time the fragile defensive line was penetrated in many places and the Germans pushed through with light machine guns. The situation was getting critical:

> I moved continually between my posts, sometimes on horseback, and sometimes on foot, and witnessed the enemy piled dead before our guns. The heaviest losses were inflicted.
>
> So critical was the situation that I used orders to my sergeants in charge of gun teams that at any time that they saw British troops retiring they were to fire on them; and from the mill I saw one of my gunners destroy a platoon of one regiment in full flight.

However, there was nothing to do but execute a tactical withdrawal to a stronger line, covered by machine-gun fire. The official war diary for April 1918 recorded:

No finer retirement could have been carried out. In the face of great enemy opposition and in the teeth of heavy machine-gun fire at its outset it was carried out without loss to either personnel or material, and every gun was withdrawn by concealed approached and with irreproachable discipline to the line … which was now held firm by a few New Zealand marksmen.

By 15 April the line was stable and by the 18th the line was firmly established and welcoming with open arms significant French reinforcement. During a reconnaissance of the front during the day, Hutchison was overcome with gas and rendered unconscious. He was missing for three days and had been reported killed in action. By the time he returned to headquarters there was a new commanding officer in his place who, being clued up on Hutchison's reputation, didn't hang around for long.

For his actions during this time Hutchison was recommended for the Victoria Cross. However, due to insufficient eyewitnesses the recommendation was turned down. He was instead awarded the DSO. The citation for which was published in the *London Gazette* on 16 September 1918:

> For conspicuous gallantry and devotion to duty at Meteren, from 12th to 17th April, 1918, while in command of three companies of machine-gunners. He drove off heavy enemy attacks with great slaughter. He handled his guns excellently, and displayed great determination and initiative under the hottest fire.

After a brief stint guarding prisoners of war in Rouen, he was demobilised with the rank of lieutenant colonel.

After the war, he worked tirelessly to further the prospects of veteran soldiers. He was chairman of the Old Contemptibles Association as well as a leading figure within the Royal British Legion. He also became more involved in general politics, running as a Liberal Democrat candidate in Uxbridge during the 1923 general election, although he was not elected. He stayed active in politics for many years, although his views became more aligned to the right wing and he even attended a number of Nuremberg rallies in the 1930s. He was also a prolific author, writing both spy novels and compiling historical records of his own and his regiments' experience. He died in 1946, aged 56.

BIBLIOGRAPHY
AND SOURCES

The details below are not necessarily 100 per cent exhaustive, but they have made up the bulk of the research material for the book. However, it is now very easy to supplement any type of research with a helping hand from Google. A quick internet search on any name or topic usually brings up an enormous amount of information and there is now a plethora of specialist sites catering for the military history geek.

The Imperial War Museum website (www.iwm.org.uk) is wonderful, as are many of the websites run by the major museums and indeed national and local newspapers. There are also some brilliant private websites, such as www.worldwar1.co.uk, www.worldwar1.com, www.firstworldwar.com, www.cwgc.org, www.hellfire-corner.demon.co.uk and www.1914–1918.net, to name but a few. Add to these the proliferation of online genealogy websites such as The National Archives, Ancestry, the Australian War Memorial, findmypast, etc. who are leading a crusade to digitise and upload as much historical documentation as possible and it quickly becomes apparent that the internet is a very potent research tool indeed. It is impossible to list every single webpage I have used but the sites I have listed above are well worth a click if the reader hasn't already done so.

John Hines

Great War Magazine, Issue 32 (Great Northern Publishing, July 2007).

Holledge, J., article in the *Sunday Mirror* (Australia), 21 July 1968.

National Archives of Australia – B2455 (First World War service records).

Louis Arbon Strange

Hearn, Peter, *Flying Rebel: The Story of Louis Strange* (HMSO, 1994).

Shores, C., Franks, N. and R. Guest, *Above the Trenches* (Grub Street, 1990).

Strange, Louis, *Recollections of an Airman* (Greenhill Books, 1989).

Kenneth Edward Brown

Harrow School, '10 April 1918 to the End of the War' in *Harrow Memorials of the Great War*, vol. VI (Philip Lee Warner, 1918).

National Archives – war diary of 2/4th Oxfordshire and Bucks – LI WO95/3067.

Petrie, F. Lorraine, *The Royal Berkshire Regiment 1914–1918* (Naval and Military Press, 2009 reprint).

Rose, Captain G.K., MC, *The Story of the 2/4th Oxfordshire and Buckinghamshire Light Infantry* (BH Blackwell, 1920).

Horace George Angier

Angier, H., *The Battalion Runner: The Short Life of H. G. Angier* (privately published, 2009).

Douie, Charles, *The Weary Road* (John Murray, 1929).

National Archives – war diary of 2nd Battalion, Royal Berkshire Regiment – WO95/1729.

Quote from 1713 Pte F. Lewis (Royal Warwickshire Regiment) taken from an interview by Tom Oates – full interview can be seen at www.hellfire-corner.demon. co.uk/runner.htm.

William Barnard Angier

Angier, Harry, *A Hussar's War* (privately published, 2006).

Durand, Sir H. Mortimer, *The Thirteenth Hussars in the Great War* (Naval and Military Press Ltd, 2003).

National Archives – war diaries – WO95/1186 and WO95/5089.

Julian Henry Francis Grenfell

The Balliol College War Memorial Book (privately published, 1924).

Bridges, Robert Seymour, *The Spirit of Man* (Forgotten Books, 2012).

Creagh, Sir O'Moore VC, *The Distinguished Service Order 1886–1923* (JB Hayward & Son, 1978).

Dictionary of National Biography 1901–1911, vol. I. – 'Sidney Lee' (Oxford University Press, 1939).

Moseley, Nicholas, *Julian Grenfell: His Life and the Times of his Death 1888–1915* (Holt, Rinehart and Winston, 1976).
Osborn, E.B., *The Muse in Arms* (Frederick A. Stokes Company, 1917).

Max Kennedy Horton

Chalmers, W.S., CBE, DSC, *Max Horton and the Western Approaches* (Hodder and Stoughton, 1954).
Compton-Hall, Richard, *Submarines at War 1939–45* (Periscope Publishing, 2004).
Creagh, Sir O'Moore, VC, *The Distinguished Service Order 1886–1923* (JB Hayward & Son, 1978).
Various, *Deeds that Thrill the Empire* (Hutchinson & Co., 1916).

Geoffrey Claude Langdale Ottley

Creagh, Sir O'Moore, VC, *The Distinguished Service Order 1886–1923* (JB Hayward & Son, 1978).
National Archives – war diary of 2nd Royal Scots Guards – WO95/1657.

Hubert William Godfrey Jones

Flight Magazine – various editions 1917–34.
Giblin, H. and N. Franks, *The Military Cross to Flying Personnel of Great Britain and the Empire 1914–1919* (Savannah Publications, 2008).

Frederick George Head

Great War Magazine (Great North Publishing).
National Archives – war diary of 1/17th London Regiment
    – WO95/2737 and WO95/2732.
Wilcox, Ron, *The Poplars* (East London History Society).

John Evelyn Carr

Great War Magazine (Great North Publishing, 2006).
Lindsay, Lt Col J.H., *The London Scottish in the Great War*
    (Naval and Military Press, 2009).
National Archives – war diary of 1st London Scottish
    Regiment – WO95/1266.

Basil Bedsmore Rackham

Imperial War Museum audio interview – Catalogue number
    15600.
Jerrold, Douglas, *The Hawke Battalion, Some Personal Records of
    Four Years 1914–1918* (The Naval and Military Press, 2006).
National Archives – war diary of Hawke Battalion –
    WO95/3114.

Frederick Watson

Great War Magazine (Great Northern Publishing).
National Archives – war diary of 2/5th Battalion King's Own
    Yorkshire Light Infantry – WO 95/3091.

Graham Seton Hutchison

Creagh, Sir O'Moore, VC, *The Distinguished Service Order 1886–1923* (JB Hayward & Son, 1978).

Hammerton, Sir John (ed.), *The Great War ... I was There!*, part 32 (1939).

Hutchison, G.S., *Footslogger, an Autobiography* (Hutchinson, 1931).

INDEX

If you enjoyed this book, you may also be interested in …

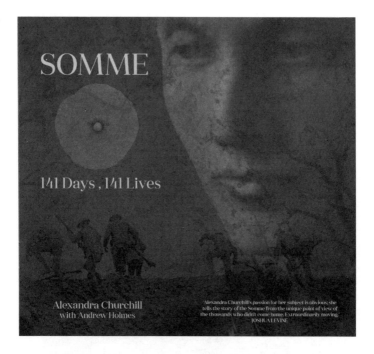

978 0 7509 6532 3

If you enjoyed this book, you may also be interested in …

PENNY STARNS

SISTERS
OF THE
SOMME

TRUE STORIES FROM
A FIRST WORLD WAR
FIELD HOSPITAL

978 0 7509 6162 2

If you enjoyed this book, you may also be interested in …

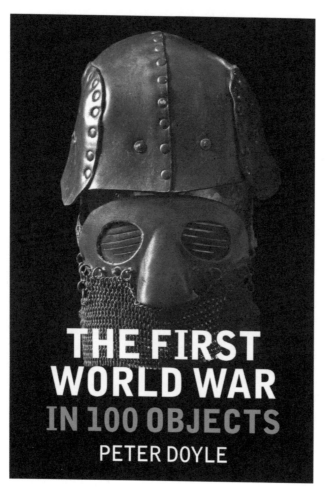

THE FIRST WORLD WAR IN 100 OBJECTS

PETER DOYLE

978 0 7509 6848 5